THE
POCKET BOOK
OF
ARSENAL

By Kevin Whitcher

With special thanks to Brian Dawes

Published by Vision Sports Publishing in 2010

Vision Sports Publishing
19-23 High Street
Kingston upon Thames
Surrey
KT1 1LL

www.visionsp.co.uk

Text © Kevin Whitcher
Illustrations © Bob Bond Sporting Caricatures

ISBN: 978-1905326-92-1

Series editor: Jim Drewett
Series production: Martin Cloake
Design: Neal Cobourne
Illustrations: Bob Bond
Cover photography: Paul Downes, Objective Image
All pictures: Getty Images

Printed and bound in China by Toppan Printing Co Ltd

A CIP catalogue record for this book is available from the British Library

THIS IS AN UNOFFICIAL PUBLICATION

All statistics in *The Pocket Book of Arsenal* are correct up until the
end of the 2009/10 season.

CONTENTS

FOREWORD BY
GEORGE GRAHAM

As a player, it was a very big culture shock joining Arsenal from Chelsea when I did in 1966. I came to a much bigger club, although underperforming, but I began to understand what professionalism they stood for, with very high standards. Twenty years later when I became manager I was ecstatic at getting the job and as I settled, realised the important position I held, looking around the place. It was full of successful history. Also, as I did a lot of travelling in the job, I had time to enjoy reading and learning about the history of the club and I built up a decent collection of old Arsenal books, going back to those written by Herbert Chapman, George Allison and David Jack.

I learned that the Gunners were one of the first English clubs to travel regularly abroad, including South America, and that Arsenal don't do things on the cheap. The stadium they built at Highbury was way ahead of its time with the two main stands, the Marble Halls and the standards of the dressing rooms. And that was back in the days before the Second World War, when it was unbelievable to think that visiting teams could come and play in this magnificent stadium. And what they've done over the last few years is the same again, building a home that is arguably the best in Great Britain and probably Europe.

I can't help but be proud of my own part in the club's history, and I wanted to win as many trophies as I could in my time as manager at Arsenal. But it was hard to think anyone could come close to what Herbert Chapman did at the club. He was ahead of his time with changes such as the white sleeves, numbers on shirts, floodlights and getting the name of the local underground station changed to Arsenal.

I am sure readers will delight in either reminiscing in or learning about the triumphs in the rich history of the club, including those in which I played a part, such as the 1971 double and the great nights at Anfield and in Copenhagen.

But to finish, I think it's time to lay to rest a myth that has grown since my days as the boss at Highbury. One day I was playing games with journalists and I told them that, being a keen gardener, when I planted my bulbs for the following spring, I placed the tulips to grow in a 4-4-2 formation and the daffodils in a 3-5-2. On a roll, I then told them I was having a swimming pool put in, with the Arsenal crest and the cannon inlaid into the tiles on the bottom! They printed it and people believed it. So much so that even now, it's amazing when people come round and they still ask to see the famous swimming pool!

So although you can't believe everything you read in the newspapers, the same cannot be said of the great story of a very special football club you will read about on the pages that follow. Enjoy.

Special thanks to George Graham, his fee for this foreword has been donated to Bob Wilson's Willow Foundation.

...CLUB DIRECTORY...

Club address: Arsenal Football Club
Highbury House, 75 Drayton Park
London N5 1BU

General club enquiries: 020 7619 5003

Fax Number: 020 7704 4001

Box Office/Ticket Info: 020 7619 5000

Dial-a-Ticket: 0844 277 3625

Match Information Line: 0844 931 2211

Stadium Tours: 020 7619 5000

Junior Gunners: 020 7619 5000

Travel Club: 020 7619 5000

Commercial & Marketing: 020 7704 4170

Corporate Hospitality:
0845 262 0001

Highbury House
Restaurant:
020 7704 4270

LIGA DE CAMPEONES
2001-2002
R.C.D. MALLORCA   ARSENAL F.C.
F.C. SCHALKE 04   GRUPO C   PANATHINAIKOS

The Armoury Shop:
  020 7704 4120
All Arsenal Shop: 020 7704 4128
Arsenal Shop at Finsbury Park:
  020 7272 1000
Arsenal Home Shopping:
  020 7619 5000
Arsenal Soccer Schools: 020 7704 4140
Arsenal in the Community: 020 7704 4140
Disability Helpline: 020 7619 5050
Arsenal Ladies: 01727 747 452
Email addresses:
General Enquiries:
    info@arsenal.co.uk
Box Office: boxoffice@arsenal.co.uk
Membership:
    membership@arsenal.co.uk
Club website: www.arsenal.com

FA CUP WINNERS
20 03
ARSENAL

CUP FINAL
Arsenal v Manchester United
Football Association Challenge Cup Competition
Saturday 12th May 1979 Kick-off 3pm
Wembley
Stadium

THE STORY OF THE GUNNERS
EARLY BATTLES
1886-1924

When Arsenal began their illustrious history in 1886, they were effectively a works team. Four friends employed at Royal Arsenal, a government munitions factory in Woolwich, south east London, decided to form the club and named it after Dial Square, one of the factory's workshops.

David Danskin was the main organiser of the quartet and raised the ten shillings and sixpence required for a football by getting some of his workmates to chip in with sixpence each. Danskin was also the club's first captain and a debut match was arranged against Eastern Wanderers. The Dial Square players provided their own kits, albeit ones of different colours. The factory was a good source of players and the opposition were beaten 6–0. This despite the pitch being somewhat unorthodox by modern standards, its shape dictated by the surrounding backyards and a ditch that was little more than an open sewer.

The team held a meeting at the Royal Oak public house soon after and agreed two significant changes. The club's name would be Royal Arsenal and their home games would be played on Plumstead Common. The nearby Star pub was used for their changing rooms and

although times moved on, a century later the concept
of an Arsenal player being in a public house in the
build-up to a match was not unheard of until the
arrival of Arsène Wenger as manager.

The team improved as some of the factory workers
Danskin recruited had experience of playing at a
higher level for clubs in both England and Scotland.
The 1890 London Charity Cup provided Arsenal's first

Workers stream away
from the main gate at
the Woolwich Arsenal
factory in south east
London, 1912

One of the earliest pictures of the club, then called Royal Arsenal, in 1888

trophy and a year later the club changed their name again, to Woolwich Arsenal.

Arsenal first entered the FA Cup in 1892, only to be knocked out by Derby County. To rub salt in the wound, Derby promptly signed two of Arsenal's

players at the end of the game! Derby were a First Division team, which left the non-league amateurs of Arsenal powerless to prevent the players from leaving – all this a hundred years before anyone had heard of Jean-Marc Bosman.

The affair prompted the club to apply to join the Football League and the application was accepted. Their first season as a fully-fledged professional league club was spent in the Second Division in 1893, ending with a ninth-place finish. By this time, they had moved to Plumstead's Invicta Ground, where they had been playing for three years. When its owner upped the annual rent from £200 to £350 as Arsenal's success grew, the club decided to buy their own ground and formed a limited liability company to raise the money to buy the Manor Ground, nearby in Plumstead. The 1,552 £1 shares were mostly bought by manual workers who lived in the local area, with not a billionaire in sight.

In 1904, less than 20 years after their formation, the team won promotion to the First Division. By this time, they were enjoying sizeable crowds, with over 25,000 turning up for one FA Cup tie. However, the club failed to push on due to financial problems, and were forced to sell some of their better players. In 1913 they eventually paid the price and were relegated back to Division Two. By this time, property magnate Sir Henry Norris had become the chairman and felt the club needed to move to a highly populated area with a good transport network. He agreed with the Church of England to buy a 21-year lease on some land they owned in Highbury, north London, very close to the Gillespie Road underground station. Despite opposition from Tottenham, Leyton Orient

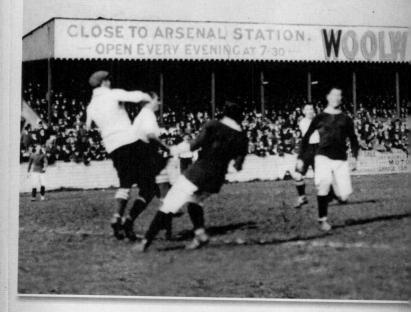

and Chelsea, the Football League decided there was nothing in their rules to prevent the move, so Arsenal became a north London club and are still regarded as arrivistes by Spurs fans to the current day.

Aside from the £20,000 cost of the lease, Norris paid £80,000 to build a stadium on the land. He needed the club to return to the top division if he was to profit from his investment. This was managed when League football resumed in 1918 after the First World War, although Arsenal's promotion to an expanded First Division was somewhat controversial, as they

An early clash with Spurs, in the 1906 Southern Charity Cup, at the Manor Ground in Plumstead

returned due to a vote amongst the league chairmen rather than their pre-war finishing position. That it was at the expense of near neighbours Tottenham Hotspur, who were relegated to Division Two at the same time, made the questionable nature of the Gunners' rise to the top flight all the sweeter. The club have never suffered relegation since.

Leslie Knighton was appointed manager in 1919, but enjoyed limited success, eventually being sacked by Norris six years later after the club had narrowly avoided relegation. His job was advertised in *Athletic News*, the description culminating in the words: "Gentlemen whose sole ability to build up a good side depends on the payment of heavy and exorbitant transfer fees need not apply." Early in the club's history, the notion of seeing good players leave and there being limited funds to build the team was already becoming familiar to Arsenal fans...

However, when the crunch came, Henry Norris realised that he had to speculate to accumulate – as he had done with the building of the stadium in Highbury. So he paid the successful manager of Huddersfield Town, Herbert Chapman, handsomely to head south and leave behind the club where he had won two league titles in succession (a third was added by the team he had built). Norris had a reputation as something of a dictator, as Knighton wrote: "Everyone was afraid of Sir Henry. And no wonder! I have never met his equal for logic, invective and ruthlessness against all who opposed

him." Chapman, aware of this, bargained hard before agreeing to take the job, and insisted on complete control over team matters as well as money to strengthen the squad. Things were going to be done differently under the new manager.

Huddersfield pinned in defence during an early game at Highbury

BADGE OF
HONOUR

Arsenal's first crest came into existence two years after the club was formed, and was very similar to the coat of arms of the borough of Woolwich in which they played, which also featured lions' heads and three upright cannons.

The club's very first crest, inspired by the Borough of Woolwich's coat of arms

The area was synonymous with the military, so it was not only its formation by workers in the Royal Arsenal armaments factory that was a factor in the choice of design. Cannons were dropped from the crest when the move to a new home north of the river took place in 1913, but only for nine years. Given the club's nickname continued to be The Gunners, it was hardly surprising that they did not remain absent for long.

The version seen on the 1935 shirt was one of several variations on the theme of a single cannon with the AFC lettering, as the crest seemed to be tweaked on an almost annual basis in the 1920s and 30s. Initially, the cannon pointed eastwards, although over the years fans were to become familiar with the westward direction seen on the 1930s versions. The frequent changes were not a cause of great controversy because the crest was rarely featured on the players' shirts except on special occasions such as

cup finals. It tended to be more a feature of the club's stationary and matchday programmes.

Captain Tom Parker in 1930, with one of a number of badge designs from the era

One version from this time that has remained popular to this day is the one which became a feature of the newly rebuilt East Stand in 1936. It was inlaid on the first floor of the stadium's Marble Halls reception, in the lobby that led to the directors' box, as well as featuring above the doorway on the exterior of the listed building. Forming the letters 'AFC', the club continue to use this on their merchandising today. The cannon had not been ignored in the design though, as this was inlaid on the floor on the ground floor and also featured outside on the façade of the art deco stand.

The 1936 crest, still in evidence today

A new crest was unveiled in 1949 that featured the Latin motto 'Victoria Concordia Crescit' (which translates as 'victory grows out

21

Adopted in 1949, this famous crest lasted 53 years and became synonymous with the club

The stripped down cannon that adorned the classic shirt of the 1970s, modelled by Charlie George

of harmony'). The design also featured the London Borough of Islington's coat of arms and the word 'Arsenal' picked out in gothic lettering. It was used for 53 years, experiencing only minor changes – mainly the colours of the various elements.

On the players' shirts, as a crest became a constant rather than occasional feature, the design was reduced to a simple cannon, as much because it was stitched in rather than being a sewn on badge. Uniformity of the official club crest and what was on the team shirts did not occur until 1990.

In 2001, the club embarked on a long-running legal case against a street trader outside the stadium who sold souvenirs with the club's crest on, and there was much debate in the courts over the legal ownership of the club's historical crests as trademarks.

Before the case was resolved, and due to

the confusion over the many different variations of
the design over the course of its history ("It's very
difficult to track back the origin of the crest and
was difficult to copyright" admitted vice-chairman
David Dein) the club decided to ensure that in
the future there would be no scope for debate by
introducing a completely new version for
the 2002/03 season.

Rather than warn fans of the
plans to make the change, the
club – having trialed ideas before
a very limited number of focus
groups – unveiled the crest
before a home league match early
in 2002. Having announced the
new design the day before, a flag
bearing it was carried around the
pitch to be received by a chorus
of boos from the Highbury crowd.
Chairman Peter Hill-Wood might have
stated, "I would like to stress that this
change is an evolution not a revolution", but
there was revolt in the air.

The initially unpopular
new design, unveiled
in 2002

It was not a good start, but the new version came
to be accepted in time and is now writ large on the
exterior of the new Emirates stadium. The cannon
points east once again whilst the Latin motto has
been dispensed with. With a much cleaner design, in
contrast to its predecessors, it is unlikely to see any
major changes.

THE INVINCIBLES

The undefeated, heavyweight champions of England parade the trophy in Islington

Between defeats to Leeds United on 4th May 2003 and Manchester United on 24th October 2004, Arsenal set a new English record of 49 consecutive unbeaten league matches. The previous best of 42, set by Brian Clough's Nottingham Forest, had spanned two seasons but did not include a complete campaign without defeat as Arsenal astonishingly achieved over the 38 fixtures of the 2003/04 Premiership season.

The team was known variously as the '49ers', the 'Unbeatables' and the 'Invincibles', after surpassing Forest's record. Clough himself described Arsenal as "nothing short of incredible," adding that they "caress a football the way I dreamed of caressing Marilyn Monroe." And it was the style with which they set the record that enhanced the achievement. A major statistical feat in itself, but to do it playing the type of football that often had opposition fans applauding them off the

field made it more remarkable still. And it became more difficult to maintain the longer it went on. "We will be a big trophy for the first team that beats us," said Wenger when the run reached 40 matches. "Every team that plays Arsenal will treat it like a cup game."

Three architects of success; icon, captain and manager

It was achieved at a time when Chelsea were spending tens of millions in the transfer market to compete with both the Highbury-based club and Manchester United (no one else had won the title for nine seasons). Such was the finance-fuelled revolution at Stamford Bridge that only something like an unbeaten season could prevent them usurping the status quo, as the subsequent two campaigns proved.

On finishing the 2003/04 league programme without a defeat, Wenger admitted, "at the beginning of this season I never felt we were capable of remaining unbeaten. I knew Chelsea had big buys and Manchester United had strengthened, and never expected us to do it."

The sequence – of 36 wins and 13 draws – was the pinnacle of four seasons in which Arsenal enjoyed five major trophies, and with only Jens Lehmann added to the 2002/03 squad of players, it proved that spending big was not always the way to achieve success. Wenger had little choice, as his budget was severely restricted by the club's need to put any income they could garner towards the building of their new stadium. The last summer in which he was able to splash significant cash was in 2001.

The Invincibles team succeeded because they mixed experience, skill,

In a great season of great performances, Henry's contribution was arguably the greatest of all

pace, flexibility and an almost telepathic understanding. All the players could chip in with goals and were comfortable in possession. The first choice eleven of Lehmann, Lauren, Toure, Campbell, Cole, Ljungberg, Vieira, Gilberto, Pires, Bergkamp and Henry was supplemented by some excellent back-up such as Keown, Parlour, Edu, Kanu and Wiltord. All international players that fitted in seamlessly when called upon. The only strengthening Wenger needed to do midway through the run was the purchase of Jose Antonio Reyes, with Wiltord out injured for several months.

"I always had that dream, and to fulfil it is marvellous," said Wenger of the unbeaten season

The players demonstrated great team spirit, both early in the run at Manchester United, when they found themselves unjustly reduced to ten men after the dismissal of Patrick Vieira but survived a last minute penalty to take a point, and at home to Liverpool several months later. Having suffered exits from the FA Cup and the Champions League in the previous week at the hands of United and Chelsea, they found themselves 2-1 down at half time and could see their title assault slipping away. In the following 45 minutes, they rallied, and won 4-2. These were both games where immense mental fortitude proved to be invaluable in the making of the Invincibles.

ARSENAL
COMIC STRIP HISTORY
1

1987... IT IS HALF-TIME IN THE LEAGUE CUP SEMI-FINAL SECOND LEG AT SPURS. ARSENAL ARE 0-2 DOWN ON AGGREGATE...

WE CAN STILL TURN THIS AROUND...

AS MANAGER GEORGE GRAHAM SPEAKS, THE PLAYERS CAN HEAR THE SPURS PA ANNOUNCER...

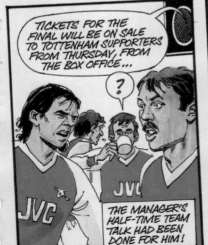

TICKETS FOR THE FINAL WILL BE ON SALE TO TOTTENHAM SUPPORTERS FROM THURSDAY, FROM THE BOX OFFICE...

THE MANAGER'S HALF-TIME TEAM TALK HAD BEEN DONE FOR HIM!

THE GUNNERS DREW LEVEL IN THE SECOND HALF BEFORE GOING ON TO WIN THE REPLAY, WITH 'ROCKY' ROCASTLE SCORING THE WINNER.

GOAL!

CUP FINAL TICKETS WENT ON SALE FROM A BOX OFFICE THREE MILES SOUTH WEST OF WHITE HART LANE!

STADIUMS

Arsenal have had several grounds in their history, but the one they called 'home' for the majority of the club's existence – from 1913 until 2006 – was officially known as 'The Arsenal Stadium'. It was rarely referred to as anything but 'Highbury' after the area of its location.

Sir Henry Norris, the chairman in 1913, relocated the club from south east London due to the urgent need to increase income. Plumstead was a tiresome journey from central London with difficult transport links, whereas Highbury was not only served by three major railway lines but also in the midst of a much better catchment area of football fans than the south east outskirts. Many local residents objected to the plan and nothing has changed in this regard, although today it can be claimed that most of them moved to the area after Arsenal Football Club so knew what to expect.

The new stadium, built on land leased from St John's College of Divinity, was designed by Archibald Leitch, the leading stadium designer of his day. Initially, Highbury featured only one wooden stand – on the east side, with the other three sides being banked terracing. The club bought the land outright in 1925, building a magnificent Art Deco-style stand designed by Claude Ferrier on the west side in 1932. Soon after, the existing East Stand was demolished so that a similar one could be built to match that opposite and subsequently the two stands were designated listed buildings due to their architectural importance.

The ends were not entirely neglected, with a roof being added to the re-terraced Laundry End, later known as the North Bank. At the same time the giant clock moved to the College End, which consequently became referred to as the Clock End.

The only significant changes until the 1980s were the reconstruction of the North Bank terrace roof after its bombing during the Second World War, the installation of floodlights in 1951, and that of undersoil heating in 1964. To the club's credit, even at the height of football hooliganism they refused

Building the terraces at the new ground in Highbury in 1913

to install perimeter fencing to prevent fans gaining access to the pitch, a move that ironically led to them not being awarded FA Cup semi-finals for a number of years.

In 1989, executive boxes were constructed above the Clock End terraces, giving partial cover to those

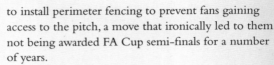

who stood below. However, the last major change to the stadium was brought about by the post–Hillsborough disaster recommendations of the Taylor Report. Stadiums had to be converted to all seating, so a new stand was built in place of the North Bank terracing. It went up over the course of the 1992/93

The 1972 FA Cup final squad line up in front of the old Clock End

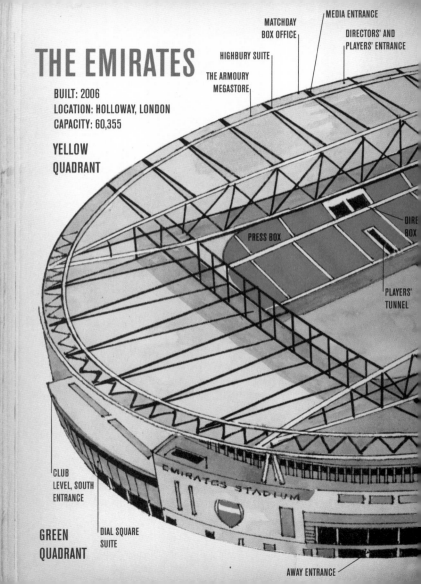

THE EMIRATES

BUILT: 2006
LOCATION: HOLLOWAY, LONDON
CAPACITY: 60,355

YELLOW QUADRANT

GREEN QUADRANT

MATCHDAY BOX OFFICE

MEDIA ENTRANCE

DIRECTORS' AND PLAYERS' ENTRANCE

HIGHBURY SUITE

THE ARMOURY MEGASTORE

PRESS BOX

DIRE BOX

PLAYERS' TUNNEL

CLUB LEVEL, SOUTH ENTRANCE

DIAL SQUARE SUITE

AWAY ENTRANCE

ORANGE QUADRANT

RED (SINGING) SECTION

ROYAL OAK SUITE

CLUB LEVEL, NORTH ENTRANCE

EMIRATES STADIUM

BLUE QUADRANT

WOOLWICH SUITE

CLUB LEVEL, EAST ENTRANCE

season, the final time that standing was allowed at the stadium, and the Clock End was converted to seating after the new stand opposite was completed. The changes meant the capacity was reduced from 55,000 to 38,500, although the stadium's record crowd of 73,295, for a match against Sunderland in 1935, was

set in the days when there was less seating.

With the increased importance of corporate hospitality and the growing popularity of both Premiership football and Arsenal, it soon became apparent that, as in 1913, the club would have to move for financial reasons. When Arsène Wenger brought sustained success to the club, it became obvious it had outgrown its home. Hemmed in by residential housing on three sides, significant expansion was inconceivable and so the directors looked at alternative locations for a new stadium.

They settled on a triangle of land housing light industrial premises and the local rubbish depot, a long goal-kick west of Highbury. The site became known as Ashburton Grove, after a road in the area. When the club received approval for its plans and raised the finance to build the new stadium, Highbury's days were numbered. The final season there was 2005/06, which culminated in a 4–2 victory over Wigan, securing Champions League football at the expense

The magnificent Art Deco facade of Highbury's East Stand

of neighbours Tottenham. It was a day that mixed exaltation with sadness. The stadium was subsequently developed into residential apartments, although the facades of the listed East and West Stands provide a permanent reminder of their previous use.

In financing their £420 million new home, the club struck a naming rights deal whereby it would be called 'The Emirates' for 15 years, promoting the eponymous middle eastern airline. Designed by HOK Sport, it was similar in look to the same company's Stadium of Light, the home of Lisbon's famous Benfica, although due to height restrictions the Emirates holds 5,000 fewer spectators, with a capacity of just over 60,000. The lower and upper tiers of the bowl-shaped stadium sandwich a middle ring that hosts 7,000 'club level' season ticket holders and 150 executive boxes. These premium-priced pews raise almost as much revenue per season as was made at Highbury from all spectators.

Supporters with memories of Arsenal's previous home bemoan the lack of atmosphere at the new ground, but the club have instigated a programme of 'Arsenalisation', decorating walls inside and out to make it feel more like home. Other differences from Highbury are that the pitch is much bigger and the fans are further from the playing surface.

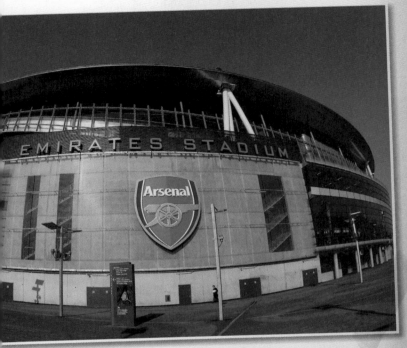

There is a perceived absence of the intimacy that was experienced before the move. However, it has been praised by football stadium expert Simon Inglis as "Britain's first truly 21st-century stadium". New memories have to be formed in the new surroundings to give fans more of a positive feeling about the place. In their first four seasons at the Emirates, Arsenal have failed to win a single major honour.

Opened in 2006, the Emirates cost £420m to build and, at 60,355, has the third highest capacity of a British football ground

GREAT GOALS

CHARLIE GEORGE
1971 FA CUP FINAL V LIVERPOOL

After a goalless 90 minutes the final came alive with a strike for each side in extra time, but with the sun mercilessly beating down it appeared as if a replay would be required to break the deadlock between the two teams.

Yet in the second period of extra time, despite looking visibly drained, Charlie George changed all that.

George Graham headed a Liverpool goal kick forward to John Radford who exchanged possession with George before teeing him up near the edge of the penalty area. "With his last ounce of energy," recalls coach Don Howe, "Charlie picks up the ball. He's about 25 yards out and I think 'He's going to have a go here'. It flew in."

George hit an unstoppable shot just inside Liverpool keeper Ray Clemence's post. The scorer himself says, "I was fortunate, I could strike a ball; 30 or 50 yards out, it didn't matter to me, I could always do that. As soon as it left my foot I knew it was a goal."

For his celebration, George laid on the Wembley turf with arms outstretched facing skywards. "He's lying on the floor, Charlie is," says Howe, "and he isn't celebrating, I'll tell you. He was well and truly knackered." Maybe so, but his work was done. Arsenal had won the 'double'.

RADFORD

GEORGE

RADFORD

GEORGE

RADFORD

LIAM BRADY
1978 FIRST DIVISION V TOTTENHAM

Christmas came early for Gooners in 1978. Two days before opening their presents, they enjoyed a five-goal win at the home of their bitter rivals, neighbours Tottenham.

The game is best remembered, despite an Alan Sunderland hat-trick, for Liam Brady's fourth goal.

As Spurs were attempting to clear their lines in the 66th minute, Brady dispossessed Peter Taylor. He had the option of passing to Frank Stapleton or using Graham Rix on his left, but with the game as good as won, he went for glory himself. He approached the edge of the Spurs box and then looped an exquisite curled shot into the keeper's top left hand corner.

BBC cameras were fortunately at the game and commentator John Motson exclaimed "Look at that. Oh, look at that," as the ball drifted into the net past the helpless Spurs defence, right in front of the ecstatic away section.

Brady's nickname was 'Chippy', although it was not derived from the technique he used to craft this goal, but rather his love of eating chips! The voting for the PFA player of the year happened soon after this match, and Brady's performance, capped off by his goal, may well have been the key factor in his winning the award when it was announced in the spring of the following year.

ALAN SUNDERLAND
1979 FA CUP FINAL V MANCHESTER UNITED

Arsenal seemed to be counting down the clock to their first trophy in eight years at 2-0 up as the final entered the final five minutes of normal time.

But a pair of quick goals from Manchester United took the wind out of Arsenal's sails and silenced the Gunners' crowd. Captain Pat Rice admits, "If the game had gone into extra time I honestly believe they would have beaten us. We were on a real downer, 2-0 up, coasting it… and all of a sudden bang, bang. We were really choked."

With a minute to go, Arsenal restarted the game after the equaliser. The ball came to Liam Brady just inside the opposition half and he began to dribble in the direction of the penalty area. He recalls, "I just wanted to get the ball in their half because I thought United were likely to score again." He slipped the ball wide to the left touchline and Graham Rix, whose pinpoint cross went over keeper Gary Bailey at the near post and fell invitingly for the onrushing Alan Sunderland. He slid the ball home past lunging defender Arthur Albiston.

From happiness to concern to depression to ecstacy – all within the space of five minutes. The goal concluded a rollercoaster of emotions for all involved both on and off the pitch.

SUNDERLAND

RIX

BRADY

BRADY

RIX

IAN WRIGHT
1993 PREMIERSHIP V EVERTON

In the latter years of the George Graham era, Arsenal often resorted to getting the ball to Ian Wright as quickly as possible as their best method of scoring goals.

Purists didn't approve, although the fans enjoyed the cup successes that prioritising the defence brought about. The approach helped Wright eventually become the leading goalscorer in the club's history, scoring many memorable goals in the process.

This one against Everton was one of his best, from an early season 2-0 Premiership victory at Highbury in which Wright netted both goals. It showed the player had a deft touch to go with his chief weapon of pace.

Gunners' keeper David Seaman launched a long clearance and the ball sailed over Kevin Campbell before bouncing into the path of Wright, who controlled it with some keepy uppy, switching it from his right to his left, dinking it into the area and leaving his hapless marker not knowing which way to turn.

Wright describes it as "my all time best goal." He remembers, "My first intention was not to do what I did in the end, but the momentum of everything took me one way, then the other, and then the ball just bounced nicely as the defender was coming to try and tackle me. And I just lifted it over Neville Southall."

TONY ADAMS
1998 PREMIERSHIP V EVERTON

Arsenal, with three Premiership matches remaining, needed to beat Everton at Highbury to celebrate their first title under Arsène Wenger in front of their home crowd.

By the time Tony Adams joined those on the scoresheet, the ephemera required for a trophy presentation was being prepared at the side of the North Bank, with the team 3-0 up.

Wenger brought on centre back Steve Bould for striker Christopher Wreh with ten minutes remaining. He took up a position in central midfield and, surprisingly, didn't look out of place. David Platt blocked an Everton move just inside his own half and the ball fell to Bould. Sensing the opportunity to break, Adams sprinted past. Bould took a couple of touches to allow his captain time to move forward, before he played a delicate chip over the advancing Everton defence. Wenger said, "I call Steve 'The Kaiser'" – after Franz Beckenbauer. His pass was worthy of the German great.

The attempt to play the offside trap failed, leaving Adams free to control the ball by knocking it down with his midriff. He says of the goal, "Although I pushed it onto my weaker left foot, the touch with my stomach was just good enough. I swung at it and the next thing I knew the net was bulging. It was a beautiful moment."

ADAMS

BOULD

PLATT

ADAMS

DENNIS BERGKAMP
2002 PREMIERSHIP V NEWCASTLE

With 28 matches of the Premiership season played, Arsenal travelled to St James' Park level on points with Manchester United at the top of the table.

Newcastle were only two points behind in fourth place. A wonder goal after 25 minutes from Dennis Bergkamp was the first in a vital 2-0 victory. Patrick Vieira won the ball and gave it to Bergkamp, deep in Arsenal's half. He hit a crossfield ball to the advancing Robert Pires, who carried it forward on the left. Meanwhile, Bergkamp made a lung-busting run towards the Newcastle area. Pires spotted him and played the ball in to his feet.

Bergkamp described the pass as being "a little bit behind me." Tightly marked by Newcastle defender Nikos Dabizas, and facing away from the goal, he took one touch with his right foot to send the ball to the defender's right, whilst spinning to run past a bemused Dabizas on his other side. He effectively collected his own pass on the goal-side of the beaten defender, and had just enough time to re-adjust his body so he could slot it home with his favoured right foot. Bergkamp explained, "It looked quite a special move but it was the most effective way. When it works out it's fantastic, but if it doesn't people would wonder why I did it."

PIRES

PIRES

BERGKAMP

BERGKAMP

THIERRY HENRY
2002 PREMIERSHIP
V TOTTENHAM

Goals against Tottenham have an extra significance for Arsenal fans. Thierry Henry's opener in this 3-0 derby victory was even more special for both the manner of the goal and its celebration.

In the 14th minute, Henry picked up a headed Patrick Vieira clearance and began a run towards the Spurs half. Closely shadowed by Matthew Etherington, his speed ended his marker's attentions as he honed in on Spurs' box. With defenders still to beat, he carried the ball across the edge of the area to set himself up for a left foot shot that beat the keeper at his near post.

BBC Radio Football Correspondent Mike Ingham summarised it thus: "Back defending initially, capturing possession, close control, pace, desire, tunnel vision, all opposition left trailing, three quarters of the length of Highbury covered, Kasey Keller helpless, North Bank End, 1-0. If that's not goal of the season, I'm looking forward to seeing the winner."

After scoring, Henry ran the length of the pitch to come to a halt on his knees in front of the away section. Encapsulating the significance of a north London derby strike, he reflected, "The goal was a good goal... especially against Tottenham." As for the celebration, "I don't know why I ran so far after the goal. I was dead for nearly two days after that."

WILTORD

HENRY

HENRY

BERGKAMP

WINNING ON ENEMY TURF

Arsenal have a unique record of winning league titles at the homes of their most intense rivals – those closest to them geographically or in the league table. It is as much of a quirk of the fixture list as anything else, as the two sides that have won more titles – Liverpool and Manchester United – have no such experiences. In 1933 and 1934, Arsenal won the title at Chelsea's Stamford Bridge. Here's the story of four of the instances in which the Gunners have landed titles at the stadiums where success tasted sweetest.

Bob Wilson jumps for joy as Arsenal clinch the first part of the 1971 double at the home of neighbours Spurs

v Tottenham, White Hart Lane, Monday 3rd May 1971

It was the lock out of all lock outs, with 51,000 inside and 100,000 unable to gain access. Arsenal were going for the league championship and FA Cup double and this, their final First Division fixture of the season, was the first trophy to be resolved. The majority of the crowd were Arsenal fans, so the atmosphere was akin to a home game. To pip Leeds United to first place, Arsenal needed either a goalless draw or a win. So when Ray Kennedy put the team 1-0 up in the 87th minute, the title was by no means secured. "That was the longest three minutes I have ever known," Kennedy later said of the period after the goal when the home side did their utmost to poop the party.

v Liverpool, Anfield, Friday 26th May 1989

Due to the Hillsborough disaster, this fixture was played almost a fortnight after the league programme should have been completed. Leaders Liverpool hosted

Adams, Hayes, Rocastle and Merson celebrate snatching the title on an unforgettable night of drama at Anfield in 1989

second-placed Arsenal in what had become a title decider. Although George Graham's team had dropped five points in their previous two matches, what is rarely remembered is that even if they had won both games, Liverpool could still have won the title by a point simply by beating the Gunners at home.

As it was, a two-goal win was required by Arsenal, but the underdogs achieved the required result, scoring twice without reply with Michael Thomas's late goal providing the most dramatic conclusion to a league season in living memory.

v Manchester United, Old Trafford, Wednesday 8th May 2002

In a reverse of the circumstances of 1971, Arsenal were attempting to win another double by claiming the Premiership title after winning the FA Cup final. Arsène Wenger's team were five points clear of United, with two matches to play. Their hosts had to win this game and hope that Arsenal might fail to beat Everton the following weekend to have any chance of overtaking them.

On paper United's chances looked to be improved by the absence of key

VISITING TEAM

019 ARSENAL
FA Barclaycard Premiership
Sat 13th April 2002 KO: 12pm
(date & kick off time to be confirmed)
Adult.   £24.00
VISITORS   01340280

East Stand Tier 1 Upper
ENTRANCE   BLOCK   ROW   SEAT
E 30   E232   8   7

vodafone

www.ManUtd.com

PLEASE TAKE UP YOUR SEAT AT LEAST 30 MINUTES PRIOR TO KICK OFF

men Adams, Henry, Bergkamp and Pires. However, it turned out to be a 90 minutes Arsenal largely controlled, sealing the title with the only goal of the game from Sylvain Wiltord after 56 minutes.

A banner in the away corner at full time said it all – 'Champions' Section'.

v Tottenham, White Hart Lane, Sunday 25th April 2004

When news filtered through before kick off that nearest challengers Chelsea had been defeated by Newcastle, Arsenal's task was clear. Avoid defeat at Spurs and they would win the title with four matches to spare.

They started by playing football of the order that had seen them reach this stage of the campaign without suffering a solitary league defeat, with collectors' item goals from Vieira and Pires in the first half.

The Gunners were cruising, but took it a little too easy and allowed Spurs back into the game. A late equaliser gave the home fans a smidgen of pride, but the afternoon – and once more the home of their local rivals – belonged to the newly-crowned champions of England.

ARSENAL
COMIC STRIP HISTORY
2

AFTER A 1970 FAIRS CUP MATCH IN ROME AGAINST LAZIO, THE PLAYERS OF BOTH TEAMS WERE INVITED TO A RESTAURANT WHERE THE VISITING PLAYERS WERE PRESENTED WITH LEATHER BAGS...

OOOOH... THAT'S NICE...

THE ARSENAL LADS STARTED THROWING THEM AROUND, AND BEFORE LONG A LAZIO PLAYER WAS HIT BY ONE, AND RETURNED IT WITH INTEREST TO BOB McNAB!

A MASS BRAWL BROKE OUT— 'LIKE THE WILD WEST' REMEMBERS FRANK McLINTOCK...

AFTER THIS INCIDENCE OF 'HANDBAGS' UEFA BANNED POST-MATCH SOCIALIZING BETWEEN TEAMS!

THE STORY OF THE GUNNERS
RISE AND FALL
1925-65

At the same time as Herbert Chapman agreed to become Arsenal's manager, the rules of the game were evolving, and a modification to the offside rule meant goals became easier to score.

Something had to be done to reduce the number the defence was conceding, and it meant changes for both Arsenal's formation and their fortunes as the new boss set to work. After a 7-0 loss to Newcastle in October 1925 a team meeting was held by the manager, with the formation changing from 2-3-5 to 3-2-5 (or 3-4-3) as a result. It was effected by playing the centre half closer to his own goal, between the two full backs, and became known as the "WM" formation. Immediately, the team's results improved as they finished the first season under Chapman as First Division runners up, behind his old side Huddersfield.

However, chairman Henry Norris refused to allow his manager to spend enough money to strengthen his team and the following season they fell away, finishing 11th. The conservatism of the club at boardroom level when it came to big money signings was to become a frequent phenomenon in Arsenal's history. The FA Cup provided some consolation, as the team made it to their first final in the competition, even if it was a disappointing day at Wembley, Arsenal losing 1-0 to Cardiff when a freak goal saw keeper Dan Lewis bundle the ball into his own net. Forward Charlie Buchan described the moment: "Lewis gathered the ball in his arms.

Captain Charlie Buchan leads the Gunners out at Highbury for the opening game of the 1925 season

As he rose, his knee hit the ball and sent it out of his grasp. In trying to retrieve it, he only knocked it further towards the goal. The ball trickled slowly but inexorably over the goal line with hardly enough strength to reach the net."

There may have been suspicions about the methods of persuasion exercised by Henry Norris to ensure Arsenal's place in the First Division after the war, but more concrete evidence of under-the-counter payments to persuade Charlie Buchan to join the club from Sunderland in 1925 eventually surfaced and the chairman was banned from football for life.

Samuel Hill-Wood succeeded Norris as chairman and both his son Denis and grandson Peter later served in the role. Chapman was given money to spend and bought the best players available to build a team that would dominate the 1930s. The moniker of 'the Bank of England' club came from this time, although future generations were to equate the idea with financial conservatism rather than having pots of money.

Arsenal's first trophy in a decade of glory was the 1930 FA Cup. A year later, they became the first southern club to win the First Division title. A second followed two seasons later when Chapman introduced white sleeves to Arsenal's red shirts, a look that has become so familiar today. The 1933 title was the first of three in a row, although Chapman tragically died of pneumonia in January 1934 so was unable to see the team he had built win a further three titles and another FA Cup before the onset of the Second World War. George Allison, also the managing director, was appointed manager to replace the departed Chapman, although he delegated the running of the team to two of his existing staff – one of whom was future manager Tom Whittaker – for the rest of the 1933/34 season.

Allison continued Chapman's work of buying players who would improve the team, with Ted Drake arriving from Southampton only two months after Chapman's death. It was an inspired buy, as his 42 goals in 41 league games helped secure another title

The Graf Zeppelin looms over Wembley as Arsenal play Huddersfield in the 1930 FA Cup final

in his first full season at the club, before he netted a club record seven in one game away to Aston Villa in December 1935. Arsenal's failure to win the title for a fourth time on the trot in 1936 was largely down to Drake missing ten weeks through a knee injury, although he returned in time to help win the FA Cup. After a fifth championship in eight seasons in

1938, only one more campaign would be completed before the onset of the Second World War, which saw eight of the club's players lose their lives on active duty.

When football recommenced, a disappointing 13th place finish in the 1946/47 table was followed by George Allison's resignation. His task was not

From left: Wilf Copping, Cliff Bastin, Eddie Hapgood, Ted Drake and George Male in 1935

helped by the retirement of some of the players who had been so instrumental in the pre-war success and, of course, the absence of those who had died in the war. Tom Whittaker stepped up from his position as first team trainer to become Arsenal's third great manager in succession. His influence was immediate and the 1948 title was landed in his first season at the helm. The club remained consistent competitors under Whittaker and made the FA Cup final in both 1950 (which they won against Liverpool) and 1952 (a defeat to Newcastle). Another league title was won in 1953.

However, Arsenal fans would have a long wait to see more silverware. The team began to decline and despite the occasional star such as Joe Baker and George Eastham, the trophies that were won by London teams were enjoyed by Tottenham, Chelsea and West Ham. Since the arrival of Herbert Chapman, Gunners' fans had never endured such lean times. Tom Whittaker died of a heart attack in 1956 and the managers that followed – Jack Crayston, George Swindin (1958) and Billy Wright (1962) – failed to bring back the good times, despite no one team dominating the 1950s and 60s. The lowpoint of this period was the attendance for a home match against Leeds United in May 1966. Whether Arsenal's 3-0 defeat or the attendance figure of a mere 4,554

spectators was more humiliating is a moot point, but
manager Billy Wright was dismissed weeks later.

His successor was found amongst the existing staff
at the club. Physiotherapist Bertie Mee was promoted
to attempt to revive Arsenal's fortunes.

Captain Joe Mercer
clutches the FA Cup
after the 1950 final win

KIT PARADE

The original Dial Square/
Royal Arsenal kit of 1886

Arsenal's humble origins meant

that for the club's very first matches, players provided their own kits, and the colours they sported did not match.

This situation only lasted until one of the players, Fred Beardsley, wrote to his old club Nottingham Forest to ask if they could help with some spare kit. He had relocated south for work, but with football more established in the north, Forest were able to donate a complete set of dark red shirts and so the development of Arsenal's kit began.

The long-sleeved shirts featured a collar and buttons down the front. They were paired with knee-length white shorts and heavy woollen red socks. This colour scheme for the shirts and shorts remained until the early 1930s (although sometimes socks changed from red to navy blue). Occasionally a club crest was sewn on the shirt for high profile matches, but there were no major changes, aside from the shade of red becoming lighter and the sometime use of a lace-up collar.

Manager Herbert Chapman, always considering innovations that would give his players an advantage, introduced hooped socks in 1932, reasoning it would help the players distinguish their team-mates more quickly.

But as far as the long-term future of Arsenal's kit was concerned, a far more significant change was to follow the next year.

Herbert Chapman introduced the white sleeves in 1933

There are two versions of how Chapman came about the idea of introducing white sleeves to the shirt. One has him playing golf with Tom Webster, a famous cartoonist of the time, who was wearing a red sleeveless sweater over a white shirt. The other has the Gunners' manager spotting someone at the ground wearing similar attire. Whichever is true, he was struck by how the combination stood out, and the red shirt with white sleeves was adopted. The kit remained as red shirt with white collar and sleeves, white shorts and hooped blue and white socks for over 20 years.

Other changes were gradual. In 1938, a few years after Chapman's death, the authorities saw the sense in his idea of numbers on the back of shirts to help identify the players. The white collar was replaced with a simple v-neck cut in the late 1950s, when lighter cotton jerseys were introduced.

Arsenal's change colours for their first

The 1950 FA Cup final gold change shirt was worn only once

few decades tended to be white shirts with black shorts. But one of the most famous away strips was that worn for the 1950 FA Cup final against Liverpool. As the two finalists wore red for their first choice kits, it was decided that both should change and manager Tom Whittaker came up with the idea for gold coloured shirts. Images of winning captain Joe Mercer with the trophy have helped give this shirt an almost mystical status, in spite of it only being worn for this match. In fact, Arsenal reverted to away kits dominated by either white or blue until the late 1960s.

The home shirt, by this time having returned to a collarless round neck, underwent a radical change between 1965 and 1967, when the white sleeves were abandoned. The attendant lack of success in this era may have been an unhappy coincidence, but when the white sleeves returned, fortunes improved. In the late 1960s a cannon logo was added to the chest, and this version of the kit, sported in the 1971 double season and the remainder of the 1970s (before the introduction of shirt sponsors and bi-annual design changes) is regarded as the classic version of the strip by most fans today. In tandem, Arsenal settled on yellow shirts and socks with blue shorts for their away colours, and despite only being utilised since 1969, the combination has come to be regarded by purists as that in which all Arsenal sides should play if a change strip is necessary.

The classic 1970s home strip

The 1980s saw changes begin to occur more rapidly. Apart from the introduction of a shirt sponsor (JVC) in 1981, the kit manufacturers (Umbro) began to feature their own logo. The replica kit market was steadily growing as fans were able to buy the shirts, which in turn fuelled more changes. Today, there are two new kits for supporters to buy each summer. Even though the home top is changed every two years, the proliferation of change strips means that kits are released which may only be worn a few times by the team, yet the profits they garner mean a big push to sell them by the club. In turn, this has led to competition between kit manufacturers for the contract to produce Arsenal's strip, with

Adidas taking over from 1986 until 1994, and Nike ever since. The sponsors changed to Dreamcast (in 1999), then O2 (2002), and since the 2006 stadium move, the Emirates airline.

As for the away shirts, the policy of continually producing different kits has led to some unusual results. In 1982, the change strip consisted of a green shirt with navy blue sleeves and shorts, whilst the socks were hooped affairs combining the two colours.

Purists favour the simple away strip introduced in 1969…

Another unusual version was the 'tractor tyre' variation on yellow and blue produced in 1991. It was such an eyesore that spectators could be forgiven for wearing sunglasses to watch the team play, although that season did mark the cannon emblem being replaced by the full club crest.

Amongst the different colours the change strips have featured since have been blue, gold, white, maroon and navy blue hoops, and good old yellow.

For the 1993 League Cup final, squad numbers

were utilised rather than the traditional numbering of a starting eleven. Additionally, the players' names were printed above their number. This innovation was also used for the FA Cup final and introduced across the Premier League the following August.

... a marked contrast with the infamous 1991 'tractor tyre' design

Highbury's final season saw the team wear a maroon (labelled 'redcurrant' for marketing purposes) and white home kit commemorating that worn in their first season there in 1913. With this exception, despite suffering a redesign every other year, the home top has remained true to the basic idea of a red shirt with white sleeves, albeit in the 2010 version with the amount of white on the sleeve being little more than a white strip. One Arsenal kit tradition that never changes is that the captain decides whether the team will wear short or long-sleeved shirts for each match.

HALL OF FAME

TONY ADAMS

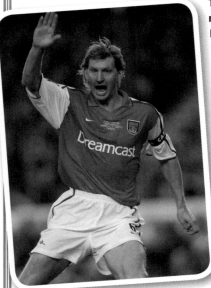

Tony Adams was Arsenal's most successful ever captain, leading the club to nine trophies over the course of three different decades.

Incredibly, before 1996, he did so in spite of the handicap of alcohol addiction, which even led to a spell in prison (after he was convicted of driving over the limit) during his second title-winning season.

An obviously talented central defender, he had all the necessary attributes from a young age to skipper the club. Even so, it came as a surprise when George Graham, following a dispute with the existing captain Kenny Sansom, handed Adams the armband at the age of 21.

It turned out to be an inspired move, as Adams proved so adept at the role he fulfilled it for three different managers.

A glut of trophies soon followed, prompted by Adams's abilities as both a defender and an organiser of others. "I've never had a problem with confidence," he revealed. It was a mindset that led him to inspire his colleagues to against-the-odds trophy-winning triumphs such as the victories at Liverpool in 1989 and against Parma five years later.

He was also chosen as skipper of England under several managers.

Arsène Wenger's arrival in 1996 gave him a new lease of life at the same time as he renounced drink. The new manager's insistence that his defenders pass the ball out rather than hoof it clear revealed Adams was more than simply a battering ram.

"I always believed I was a bloody good footballer," he said in 1997. "Now I'm playing without fear."

Added to the fresh approach to the physical preparation of players, it extended Adams's career long enough for him to inspire the Gunners to a pair of league and cup doubles before the man George Graham dubbed "a colossus"called it a day in May 2002. He was the definitive one-club man, although ultimately that proved to be thanks to Wenger.

"He's a pure joy to work for," enthused Adams in 2000. "I play for him now and if I didn't have him I wouldn't be at Arsenal."

> **The Arsenal back four were all university graduates in the art of defending. I consider Tony Adams to be a professor of defence. He is simply outstanding**
>
> Arsène Wenger

Born: Romford, Essex, 10th October 1966

Arsenal appearances: 669

Arsenal goals: 48

Honours won with Arsenal:
League Championship (1989, 1991), Premiership (1998, 2002), European Cup Winners' Cup (1994), FA Cup (1993, 1998, 2002), League Cup (1987, 1993)

Other clubs: None

International appearances: England, 66 caps, 5 goals

TONY ADAMS FACTFILE

CLIFF BASTIN

Cliff Bastin only appeared for his local club Exeter for one season, during which he was spotted by Herbert Chapman and brought to Arsenal, aged 17, in 1929.

Given the nickname 'Boy Bastin' for obvious reasons, he demonstrated coolness and accuracy in front of goal, assets he would utilise when he became the team's penalty taker.

Played mostly as a left winger at Arsenal, one of the reasons he was a prolific scorer was Chapman's instruction that wide players were to cut in rather than hug the wings, and the supply of chances forged by the play of Alex James ensured Bastin enjoyed plenty of opportunities. He frequently took a position ten yards in from the touchline, cognisant of what James was likely to do.

Bastin played a part in all of the trophies won by the club during the 1930s, going on to become Arsenal's record goalscorer, a distinction he held for 58 years until Ian Wright finally overtook his tally in 1997. He also enjoyed international success with England during the 1930s, making his debut at the age of 19.

After finishing top scorer for his club in 1932/33 and 1933/34, Bastin was usurped in the goals scored table when Ted Drake arrived at Arsenal.

Bastin was played in other positions in seasons the team failed to win the league. When he was moved back to his favoured position in 1937/38, Arsenal won the title again, in no small part thanks to the increase in Bastin's goal tally.

Injury to his right leg meant he was absent for much of the following season, before the war interrupted his career at a time (aged 27) he should have been reaching his peak.

Bastin's increasing deafness meant he was excused military service, and so he served in the war as an air raid warden, ironically stationed at the top of the Highbury Stadium with future Arsenal manager Tom Whittaker. He played wartime football (making around 250 appearances) to keep up the morale of civilians, yet his leg never fully recovered and after the war he played only seven more times for the club, before retiring in 1947 and returning to Exeter to run a pub.

> **Cliff Bastin had a trait few of us are blessed with, an ice-cold nerve**
> Tom Whittaker

CLIFF BASTIN FACTFILE

Born: Exeter, Devon, 14th March 1912

Arsenal appearances: 396

Arsenal goals: 178

Honours won with Arsenal:
League Championship (1931, 1933, 1934, 1935, 1938), FA Cup (1930, 1936)

Other clubs: Exeter City (1928)

International appearances: England 21 caps, 12 goals

DENNIS BERGKAMP

Dennis Bergkamp's signing in 1995 signified the moment that Arsenal declared their ambitions to become one of the top teams in world football.

He was the kind of undisputed international superstar who excites supporters into a frenzy before he has even kicked a ball. Although the player had not enjoyed a happy time while at Inter Milan, his reputation as a visionary who made the game look easy remained undiminished when he arrived in north London.

He played as a shadow striker behind an out and out forward, initially Ian Wright, then Nicolas Anelka and finally Thierry Henry. His tactical awareness and deft passes meant he was ideally suited to play 'in the hole'. From there, he scored some memorable goals and set up countless others.

As he became settled, the team's league position improved. Fifth in his first season, third in his second (after

Wenger's arrival) and champions in 1997/98, when he also won both the Footballer of the Year and Players' Player awards.

At the beginning of that season, Wenger said: "Can you say Bergkamp is not the best player in the world right now? If there is better, I have not seen him." Gooners simply called him 'God'.

"Dennis is the best player I have ever played with as a partner. It is a dream for a striker to have him in the team with you"
Thierry Henry

His presence was vital in attracting others to the club. He reflected after the first Premiership title, "I was part of the start and then the boss came, Vieira, Petit, Overmars and then on to this team where they're basically all world-class players. Maybe 15 years ago they wouldn't have played for Arsenal, but they do now and I helped that."

If he was like a magnet to other players, it was nothing compared to his effect on the fans. He was big box office, as 'Sold Out' signs became the order of the day.

In spite of his playing well into his thirties, he remained a key man in the five trophy victories between 2002 and 2005, before bowing out at the end of Highbury's final season.

That it was his testimonial game which opened the new stadium proved a fitting tribute to an Arsenal legend.

Born: **Amsterdam, Holland**, 10th May 1969

Arsenal appearances: 424

Arsenal goals: 120

Honours won with Arsenal: **Premiership** (1998, 2002, 2004), FA Cup (2002, 2003, 2005)

Other clubs: Ajax (1986), Inter Milan (1993)

International appearances: Holland, 79 caps, 37 goals

DENNIS BERGKAMP FACTFILE

LIAM BRADY

Liam Brady was a midfield maestro who lit up the Gunners in a period of relative gloom – the mid to late 1970s.

He came into the side during a period when Arsenal flirted with relegation. However, the arrival of Terry Neill as manager and the return of Don Howe as coach improved things as Brady's game itself developed, with the club reaching four cup finals over three seasons from 1978 to 1980. The Irishman possessed an abundance of skill and was an adept reader of the game. Despite his relatively scrawny physique, he was deceptively strong and difficult to dispossess, especially when dribbling through opponents.

Pat Rice, captain during the latter part of Brady's Arsenal career, remembers, "The lower half of his body was so strong he just ghosted past people." And he had such a quick brain that he could either play people in, play one-twos, float a ball in or score tremendous goals himself. Indeed, as well as enjoying the ability to set up team-mates, Brady's sweet left foot ensured 'Chippy', as he was nicknamed, chipped in with his share of goals. His talent for striking a ball with minimal backlift often made it difficult for rivals to predict his intentions before he released the ball.

> ❝ There was never any doubt he would be a great because not only did he want to be a fine player, he wanted to win ❞
> Don Howe

Yet only one of the four cup finals he played in ended in victory, the 1979 FA Cup won thanks to a last-minute goal against Manchester United. Brady played a key part in the creation of all three Arsenal strikes that afternoon. The same season he was awarded the PFA Players' Player of the Year award.

But as the leading light in a team that never looked like seriously challenging for the league title, he grew frustrated and the club agreed to let him go in 1980.

He moved to Italian giants Juventus, whom he had performed against so admirably in the victorious European Cup-Winners' Cup semi-final. Unfortunately, Brady could not give Arsenal fans a happy ending to his time at Highbury, missing a penalty in the shoot-out against Valencia in the subsequent final.

LIAM BRADY FACTFILE

Born: Dublin, 13th February 1956

Arsenal appearances: 306

Arsenal goals: 59

Honours won with Arsenal: FA Cup (1979)

Other clubs: Juventus (1980), Sampdoria (1982), Inter Milan (1984), Ascoli (1986), West Ham (1987)

International appearances: Republic of Ireland, 72 caps, 9 goals

THIERRY HENRY

Nicolas Anelka's 1999 move to Real Madrid netted a £22 million fee which paid for Arsenal's state of the art training centre and a certain Thierry Henry.

Arsène Wenger quickly set about transforming the speedy winger into a centre forward, and by the time he left for Barcelona eight years later, Henry had been voted the greatest ever Gunner in a club website poll of supporters.

He played the game with power, pace, precision and at times, total freedom of expression, making him almost impossible to shackle. As Everton boss David Moyes succinctly put it, "Henry occupies all the players at the back on his own."

He was surrounded by the talents of superstar team-mates and, if anything, the five trophies in four seasons from 2002 were an underachievement from a team that was unquestionably the best in England at the time. Over this period, despite never actually winning any of the various individual prizes for a specific season, many neutrals believed Henry to be the best player in world football. The sight of the number 14 being applauded off the pitch by opposition fans when the Gunners played away was not unusual.

> ❛❛ **He'll go down in the history not only of Arsenal but of football** ❜❜
>
> Arsène Wenger

After Patrick Vieira's departure, he was made club captain for the final season at Highbury (scoring the last ever goal there) and the first campaign at the Emirates. In October 2005 away to Sparta Prague he converted twice to replace Ian Wright as the club's all-time record goalscorer. His goals were rarely mundane, sometimes almost works of art.

Henry encapsulated the perfect footballer for the manager, combining his multifarious abilities with the right attitude. The striker said of his approach, "When I am on the pitch, I will give it 100 per cent. You can never doubt my commitment. I play with my heart."

In his initial season as skipper he led the team to their first ever Champions League final, where he gallantly attempted to win the game for ten man Arsenal as a lone striker in a performance that was all about character.

THIERRY HENRY FACTFILE

Born: Les Ulis, Essonne, France, 17th August 1977
Arsenal appearances: 370
Arsenal goals: 226
Honours won with Arsenal:
Premiership (2002, 2004),
FA Cup (2002, 2003, 2005)
Other clubs: Monaco (1994),
Juventus (1999), Barcelona
(2007)

International appearances:
France, 118 caps, 51 goals

ALEX JAMES

Herbert Chapman signed inside forward James from Second Division Preston in 1929.

The previous year, he had come to the attention of leading clubs due to a brace of goals as Scotland's famous 'Wembley Wizards' demolished England 5-1 at the stadium.

The maximum wage, set by the Football League at the time, was £8 a week but the player was unhappy with this at Preston, not least because other clubs had found a way round the rule. So Arsenal arranged for leading department store Selfridges to employ him as a 'sports demonstrator' for £250 a year.

On the field, he had to adapt to a deeper role at Highbury, playing as a link man to create chances for others in the 3-4-3 system that Chapman was honing. He found it difficult initially and was dropped from the starting line-up.

He returned in time for the 1930 FA Cup final and his contribution was key. For the opening goal in the 2-0 victory over Huddersfield, he took a quick free kick, executing a one-two with Cliff Bastin before rocketing the ball into the net against an unprepared defence.

"It was one of the smartest moves ever made in a big match and it gave us the Cup," said team-mate Eddie Hapgood.

Arsenal won four titles between 1931 and 1935, and it was no coincidence that the one time they narrowly missed out (in 1932) James missed the run-in due to a serious knee ligament injury. His value to the team in his deep creative position was summed up by Matt Busby, then a player with Manchester City. "The number of goals created from rearguard beginnings by Alex James were the most significant factor in Arsenal's greatness," said Busby.

His trademark look was baggy shorts – sported to hide the long johns he wore to keep warm (he suffered from rheumatism) – and a distinctive heavily-gelled centre parting. He captained the side to the final honour he would win with the club, the 1936 FA Cup, beating Sheffield United.

A year later he retired, arguably the most important player in Arsenal's dominance of the decade.

> **ff Alex James was widely regarded as the most astute football tactician of his time JJ**
> Stanley Matthews

Born: Mossend, Lanarkshire, 14th September 1901

Arsenal appearances: 261

Arsenal goals: 27

Honours won with Arsenal: League Championship (1931, 1933, 1934, 1935), FA Cup (1930, 1936)

Other clubs: Raith Rovers (1922), Preston North End (1927)

International appearances: Scotland, 8 caps, 3 goals

ALEX JAMES FACTFILE

JOE MERCER

Joe Mercer was brought from Everton in November 1946 at a time when Arsenal were languishing in 21st place in the First Division table.

His arrival transformed the team and he was made temporary captain at the start of his first full season. When club captain Leslie Compton returned from his cricketing duties after the Gunners had made a blazing start, he insisted Mercer remain skipper. They went on to secure the league championship, with Mercer's experience of winning the title with Everton in 1939 undoubtedly a key asset.

Although an attack-minded left half at his previous club, he was converted to a more defensive role at Highbury. However, his domestic circumstances remained unaltered, as he was allowed to live and train on Merseyside, only joining up with his team-mates on matchdays.

In 1950, he led the team to a successful FA Cup final against Liverpool, and was voted Footballer of the Year that season. Although a second FA Cup final appearance – against Newcastle – two years later ended in disappointment, a second title under his captaincy followed in 1953.

Fellow post-war great Len Shackleton believed "Joe Mercer, as an Arsenal player between his 30th and 40th birthdays, was a far better wing half than in his younger days. When he discovered his legs would not allow him to run all over the field, and played almost entirely in his own half, he was great. The service of wonderful passes that flowed from this spindly bow-legged genius was, I am certain, 50 per cent of the reason for Arsenal's post-war successes."

His ability to intercept and distribute was key, in tandem with his shrewd tactical knowledge and a talent to inspire confidence in his team-mates.

Mercer decided to retire in May 1953, but changed his mind and returned to the game, lining up to help Arsenal as they tried to defend their title.

However, in April the following year he had no option but to call time on his playing career, suffering a broken leg after colliding with a colleague in a match against Liverpool.

> **Joe Mercer was a tremendous tackler, timing his interventions perfectly. He had a deceptive speed**
> Tommy Lawton

Born: Ellesmere Port, Cheshire, 9th August 1914
Arsenal appearances: 275
Arsenal goals: 2
Honours won with Arsenal: League Championship (1948, 1953), FA Cup (1950)
Other clubs: Everton (1932)
International appearances: England, 5 caps, 0 goals

JOE MERCER FACTFILE

FRANK McLINTOCK

Frank McLintock was one of a number of great Arsenal captains. He joined the club from Leicester City in 1964, and was made skipper in 1967.

A natural for the job, he recalls, "I was very good at sorting people out, pushing them around, exaggerating praise for people. It never entered my head that I shouldn't tell someone what they should be doing."

The Gunners were in the process of transformation and success beckoned with two consecutive League Cup final appearances at the end of the sixties. However, after winning neither (making him a four-time Wembley cup final loser), the disheartened captain handed in a transfer request.

Coach Don Howe persuaded McLintock to remain and had the idea of converting him from central midfield to the heart of the defence the following season. Despite his relative lack of height for the position, it proved an inspired switch. He demonstrated an excellent reading of the game and a cool head, without losing the infectious passion that at times in midfield meant he tried to do too much.

A first trophy in 18 seasons followed, as Arsenal won the Fairs Cup, in no small part thanks to the captain's rousing of his players after the final first leg defeat away to Anderlecht.

> **He was a great leader, an inspiration. He could pick everybody up or give them a rollicking when they needed it**
>
> Jon Sammels

But better was to come in 1970/71 with honours for both man and club as he led the Gunners to the League Championship and FA Cup double and took the Footballer of the Year award.

The experience of losing his first four finals at Wembley meant he refused to let the opportunity to win one go easily, and once again he rallied his troops when Liverpool took an extra time lead in the 1971 FA Cup final. "Come on, we can still win it!" he roared, as the final 2-1 scoreline to Arsenal confirmed.

Despite narrowly failing to successfully defend either trophy in 1972, manager Bertie Mee allowed McLintock to leave the club for Queens Park Rangers a year later. It was a mistake that signaled the end of a golden Gunners era.

Born: Glasgow, 28th December 1939

Arsenal appearances: 403

Arsenal goals: 32

Honours won with Arsenal: European Inter-Cities Fairs Cup (1970), League Championship (1971), FA Cup (1971)

Other clubs: Leicester City (1957), Queens Park Rangers (1973)

International appearances: Scotland, 9 caps, 1 goal

FRANK McLINTOCK FACTFILE

PATRICK VIEIRA

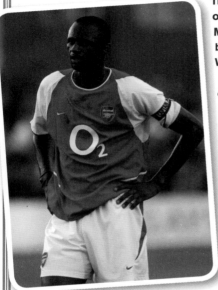

The purchase of the 20-year-old Patrick Vieira from AC Milan in 1996 signaled the beginning of the Arsène Wenger era at Arsenal.

Although not officially confirmed as manager, Wenger instructed the club to buy the central midfielder as he was on the verge of signing for Ajax. It proved one of the finest pieces of business the club has ever done. He made an immediate impression, coming on as a sub against Sheffield Wednesday to boss the midfield and turn the match around. He became a fixture in the team and the following season his partnership with fellow Frenchman Emmanuel Petit provided a bedrock that enabled the club to win the Premiership and FA Cup double. The season was capped by the two men combining for Petit to score France's third and last goal in the World Cup final against Brazil.

Vieira combined an athleticism that allowed him to get from box to box at pace with an uncanny ability to retain possession in the tightest of situations, frequently drawing free-kicks from frustrated opponents. Both a ballwinner and a distributor, he was a vital cog and the team never looked quite as effective in his absence. He became vice-captain to Tony Adams and due to injuries the skipper suffered in his final season – when the club recorded a second 'double' under Wenger – Vieira ended up leading the team more frequently than Adams.

ff Patrick was one of the greatest players in the club's history. His impact, not only at Arsenal but in English football overall, was tremendous
Arsène Wenger **JJ**

He was given the armband in his own right when Adams retired and there followed three consecutive trophy-winning seasons under the inspirational number 4, including the 'Invincibles' Premiership crown of 2003/04. Lee Dixon said of his influence on the squad, "They look up to him for his performances, but he is also the man to link the foreign players with the French and English players. He holds it all together." His last kick for the Gunners was the winner in the penalty shoot-out to decide the 2005 FA Cup final against Manchester United. With his departure the trophies dried up as Arsenal failed to successfully replace the man from Senegal.

Born: Dakar, Senegal, 23rd June 1976

Arsenal appearances: 406

Arsenal goals: 34

Honours won with Arsenal: Premiership (1998, 2002, 2004), FA Cup (1998, 2002, 2003, 2005)

Other clubs: Cannes (1993), AC Milan (1995), Juventus (2005), Inter Milan (2006), Man City (2010)

International appearances: France, 107 caps, 6 goals

PATRICK VIEIRA FACTFILE

IAN WRIGHT

Ian Wright was brought to Arsenal early in September 1991 and scored a hat-trick on his league debut versus Southampton, before claiming the Golden Boot award that season with 29 league goals (five scored with Crystal Palace, for whom he started the campaign).

The 29th goal, that completed a hat-trick (ironically against Southampton), was the final one scored in front of the standing North Bank.

His prolific ability to find the net (he was the club's leading scorer for six consecutive campaigns) signaled a change in Arsenal's playing style as more creative players were sacrificed by boss George Graham in order for the team to play to Wright's strengths – his pace and lethal finishing. By concentrating on defence, the team became very difficult to score against and matches were often won thanks to Wright's goals. In his second season, he helped the club to win a domestic cup 'double'.

A year later, he cruelly missed the 1994 European Cup-Winners' Cup final triumph, due to suspension. His sheer enthusiasm led to a yellow card in the semi-final second leg. He explained, "When I get into trouble on the pitch I'm so psyched up, wound up and pumped up because I want to do well, it overflows." Wright's personality was both loud and infectious and fans warmed to his demonstrative character. He wore his heart on his sleeve, a typical comment that sums up both a striker's mentality and the man's personality being when he admitted, "I'm desperate for goals: they're what my job is all about, and if I'm not scoring – even if the team is winning – I sulk."

He played for two seasons under Arsène Wenger, scoring his 179th Arsenal goal during the second to break the club's goalscoring record held by Cliff Bastin. However, he became injured in January 1998 and although his contribution to the League title that was secured four months on is undeniable, his absence demonstrated that the team could flourish without him and, at the age of 34, the manager decided Wright was dispensable.

> **He's an instinctive player. His movements are perfect, so intelligent even when he has not got the ball. And that is why he scores the goals**
> Arsène Wenger

Born: Woolwich, London, 3 November 1963
Arsenal appearances: 288
Arsenal goals: 185
Honours won with Arsenal:
Premiership (1998), FA Cup (1993), League Cup (1993)
Other clubs: Crystal Palace (1985), West Ham (1998), Celtic (1999), Burnley (2000)
International appearances: England, 33 caps, 9 goals

IAN WRIGHT FACTFILE

CHAPMAN THE INNOVATOR

Herbert Chapman was one of the greatest innovators in the game's history, and in less than a decade at Arsenal came up with several ideas which verify him as a football thinker years ahead of his time.

One of his most famous developments came very soon after his arrival at Highbury, when the team changed from the 2-3-5 formation to 3-4-3. A change in the offside law reducing the number of opposition players needed between the attacker and the goal line from three to two led Chapman to introduce a centre back to counter the opposing centre forward. The WM, as the formation came to be known, also allowed a greater balance between offensive and defensive play.

Chapman shaped not only Arsenal, but the game itself

Other ideas soon followed. In August 1928, Arsenal were the first team to wear numbers on the back of their shirts. Chapman reasoned that if players were able to identify each other more quickly, it would speed moves up. However, it did not curry favour at the Football League, and after sporting numbers for a solitary match, the club was banned from repeating the experiment.

Chapman regarded the approach of those that

ran the game as a huge cause of frustration. He wrote, "I appeal to the authorities to release the brake which they seem to delight in jamming on new ideas… as if wisdom is only to be found in the council chamber... I am impatient and intolerant of much that seems to me to be merely negative, if not actually destructive, legislation."

He advocated goal judges to decide on the issue of whether a ball actually crossed the goal line, a debate that continues to this day. He asserted, "We owe it to the public that our games should be controlled with all the exactness that is possible." He also advocated use of a white ball so that spectators could make it out more clearly.

Chapman, far right, shoots a round of golf with some of his Gunners in 1929

With Alex James, right, on the pitch at Wembley before the 1932 FA Cup final

Floodlit football was another innovation that was only adopted years later. Chapman had lights built into the West Stand to facilitate evening matches, but the Football Association insisted they could not be used for official matches. And thanks to Chapman, years before European competition, Arsenal were the first English team to regularly travel abroad to take part in showpiece friendlies, notably against Paris's Racing Club de France, who were first played in 1930.

Looking back, the suggestions seem eminently sensible, but Chapman's ideas were regarded as eccentric and off the wall in his own lifetime.

His team-talks were also revolutionary, as he encouraged players to contribute by expressing their own views. It was from this approach that the WM formation was developed. Chapman used a magnetic table on which a football pitch was marked out with tiny players that could be moved around. With the two-way discussion, all aspects of the forthcoming game were fully explored and every player was certain what would be required of them and what they might expect. The *Daily Mail* wrote of Chapman's approach, "Breaking down old traditions, he was the first club manager who set out methodically to organise the winning of matches."

More specific to his own club, Chapman introduced the now famous white sleeves to Arsenal's kit in 1934. Also, he introduced the idea of a giant clock for spectators to monitor how much of a match had been played and remained, leading to the labelling of Highbury's South Stand as the Clock End.

One proposal that was to go down in north London football folklore was to change the name of the underground station next to the club's Highbury Stadium from Gillespie Road to Arsenal. It was no small feat to persuade London Transport to effect the change, with all the signage that would need to be altered. Even today, after the stadium move, more people use Arsenal underground station to travel to home matches than any other. The legacies of football's great ideas man linger on over 70 years after his death.

Sir Jacob Epstein's bronze bust resided in Highbury for years, and it now adorns the Emirates' reception

THE STORY OF THE GUNNERS
GREATNESS BECKONS
1966-95

When Bertie Mee took over as manager in 1966, he inherited a squad of mainly young home-grown players who would bring success back to the club for the first time since the days of post-war austerity.

Although not regarded as a footballing mastermind, Mee's astute choice of first team coaches, Dave Sexton and later Don Howe, ignited the team. Under Mee, Arsenal once again reached Wembley, making it to the League Cup final two years running. In 1968 they lost to Leeds United, but were hot favourites against third division Swindon Town a year later. The Wembley pitch, however, had been reduced to a quagmire by the Horse of the Year show the previous week, and this combined with a flu epidemic at Highbury meant Arsenal failed to match their opponent's stamina on a heavy pitch, especially during extra time where Swindon ran out worthy 3-1 winners.

However, what followed proved the character of Mee's players. They reached the two-legged final of the Inter Cities Fairs Cup (soon to be re-branded the UEFA Cup) in 1970 against Belgium's Anderlecht. They were 3-0 down in the first leg in Brussels but a late consolation goal gave the team some hope. In the return leg at Highbury Arsenal needed a two-nil victory to win on away goals but an emphatic 3-0 triumph, reckoned by many to be the greatest night the old stadium ever witnessed, saw them home in style. A 17-year wait for a trophy was finally at an end.

More success came in 1970/71 as the club landed
the double of League championship and FA Cup. The
campaign culminated with the Gunners taking the
First Division title courtesy of a 1-0 win at the home
of neighbours Tottenham, thanks to a late Ray
Kennedy header. Five days later the FA Cup final
against Liverpool saw Wembley prove a happy
hunting ground, even if it needed extra time to win

Physio Bertie Mee
puts the players
through their paces in
a 1962 session
at Highbury

Celebrations after the
thrilling FA Cup final
victory over Manchester
United in 1979

the game. The attempt to defend the cup ended in a losing final appearance against Leeds in 1972, before Mee began to break up the double team, many felt too early. When the team narrowly avoided relegation in 1976, it was followed by Mee's resignation after a decade in the job.

The next manager, former captain Terry Neill, had been doing the job at Tottenham for two seasons. By this time the club's youth policy had produced a trio of good Irish players – Liam Brady, Frank Stapleton and David O'Leary. Neill brought both Pat Jennings and Willie Young with him from Tottenham and the team were soon reaching cup finals again – four between 1978 and 1980. Three were consecutive FA Cup final appearances, although the only victorious one was in 1979 against Manchester United. The 1979/80 season was especially cruel. Due to replays, the team played 70 matches that season. Four days after failing to retain the FA Cup against West Ham, they travelled to Brussels for the European Cup Winners' Cup final. A tight game against Valencia ended goalless but was lost in a penalty shoot-out.

The fans would have to wait seven years before another final appearance, as Neill allowed key players to leave, including Brady and Stapleton.

Neill was sacked in 1983 and coach Don Howe promoted. He failed to improve the team's fortunes

and resigned in 1986 when he got wind that the club were trying to recruit Barcelona boss Terry Venables to replace him. That summer, it was former player George Graham that arrived instead.

Having impressed at Second Division Millwall, he gradually cleared most of the experienced stars from the club's books to ensure his authority was not

challenged by dissenting voices, with only David O'Leary remaining at the club from among the older heads. It paid dividends as Graham inherited a good crop of talent developed at the club, augmented by bargain signings from the lower divisions and less glamorous First Division opponents.

Silverware arrived in his first season via the League

Michael Thomas scores the famous last-gasp goal that secured the title at Anfield in 1989

Ian Wright celebrates in typical style after scoring in the 1993 FA Cup final

Cup, when firm favourites Liverpool were beaten by their much less experienced rivals. It was to provide a springboard for an even more significant game two years later, when the final fixture of the season saw Arsenal visit Liverpool needing to win by a two-goal margin to pip their hosts to the title. As the home team had dominated football for 15 years, few gave Graham's young team much chance. However, they bucked the odds to become champions in dramatic fashion, scoring the decisive second goal in the 90th minute.

Two years on another championship followed,

when Arsenal lost only one of their 38 matches. It was to be the team's final serious assault on the title under Graham, as they lacked consistency and changed their style to rely more on defence than creativity. Flair players were dropped, then sold, with the manager favouring a long ball game to create chances for new signing Ian Wright. The Gunners became more adept at cup football, if only because they were very difficult to beat in tight one-off matches.

A League Cup and FA Cup double was achieved in 1993, in both instances against Sheffield Wednesday, the FA Cup final involving a replay and extra time before a late winner for the Gunners as a penalty shoot-out beckoned.

A year later, Arsenal triumphed 1-0 in the European Cup Winners' Cup final, despite being underdogs against the holders, Italian side Parma. It was a dogged defensive display that epitomised what Arsenal had become.

Despite the cup successes, the team was in decline. The following season, when evidence came to light that Graham had been receiving some of the transfer fees that the club had paid to buy players, via a Norwegian agent, he was sacked. It was an echo of what had occurred in the 1920s with chairman Sir Henry Norris. Assistant Stewart Houston took over as caretaker boss and guided the team to another Cup Winners' Cup final, but this time, Arsenal were the victims of a late winner, scored by Spanish side Real Zaragoza.

ARSENAL COMIC STRIP HISTORY 3

IN THE LAST SEASON BEFORE WORLD WAR ONE, BOTH CHELSEA AND SPURS FINISHED IN THE RELEGATION POSITIONS IN DIVISION ONE...

BOTTOM...

	P	W	D	L	F	A	Pts.
		11	8	15	64	62	30
	38	9	12	17	46	65	29
Manchester U.	38	8	13	17	51	90	28
Chelsea	38	8	12	18	57	90	28
Tottenham H.							

TOP OF... DIVISION 2

	P	W	D	L	F	A	Pts.
Derby Co.	38	23	7	8	71	33	53
Preston N.E.	38	20	10	8	61	42	50
Barnsley	38	22	3	13	51	51	47
Wolverhampton W.	38	19	7	12	77	52	45
Birmingham	38	17	9	12	62	39	43
Arsenal	38	19	5	14	69	41	43
	38	19		14	65	54	43

WHEN FOOTBALL RESUMED AFTER THE WAR, IT WAS DECIDED TO EXPAND THE FIRST DIVISION FROM 20 TEAMS TO 22...

SO... CHELSEA WILL NOT BE RELEGATED.

BUT SPURS?

ARSENAL'S SIR HENRY NORRIS 'PERSUADED' HIS FELLOW CHAIRMEN...

...THAT ARSENAL AND **NOT** SPURS SHOULD BE GIVEN A PLACE IN THE TOP FLIGHT. SPURS CLAIMED THAT **BRIBERY** WAS THE ONLY EXPLANATION FOR THEIR NEIGHBOURS' PROMOTION TO THE TOP DIVISION, WHERE THEY HAVE REMAINED EVER SINCE...

TACTICS

HERBERT CHAPMAN'S WM

In 1925, a change to the offside rule meant that only two opposing players (it had been three) were required to be between the most forward attacker and the goal to avoid being offside. As a consequence, many more goals were scored. In a team meeting after a 7-0 defeat, forward Charlie Buchan suggested, "Why not have a defensive centre half, or third full back, to block the gap down the middle?" Herbert Chapman shaped the future of football by adopting the idea and changing the traditional way teams of the time lined up.

So whereas 2-3-5 utilised two defenders and five forwards, the new 3-4-3 formation, which became known as the WM formation because of the shape of the team, offered an extra player in between the two full backs, making it more difficult for opposing forwards to score. Effectively, the centre half was moved back from midfield to become a centre back. Additionally, Chapman moved his two inside forwards deeper to provide a link between the five defensive-minded outfield players and those in attack.

As that would have left the centre forward isolated, the two wingers each moved a few yards inside, no longer hugging the touchline and looking to cut in when they received the ball (often from an inside forward during a lightning counter attack) rather than head for the goal-line to get in a cross.

The benefits for Arsenal came gradually, as Chapman honed the system and improved the quality of the players used via the transfer market. However, the glut of honours that the 1930s produced proved that 3-4-3 was the way forward and it was soon embraced by other clubs.

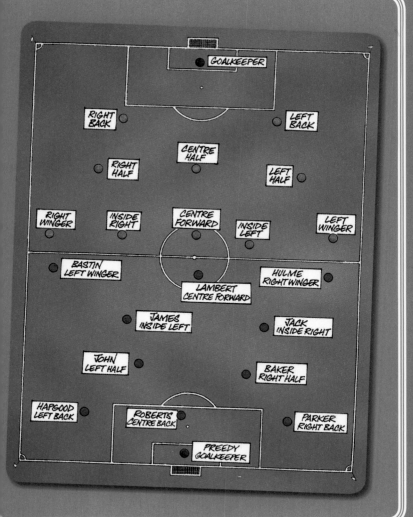

GOALKEEPER

RIGHT BACK

LEFT BACK

CENTRE HALF

RIGHT HALF

LEFT HALF

RIGHT WINGER

INSIDE RIGHT

CENTRE FORWARD

INSIDE LEFT

LEFT WINGER

BASTIN LEFT WINGER

HULME RIGHT WINGER

LAMBERT CENTRE FORWARD

JAMES INSIDE LEFT

JACK INSIDE RIGHT

JOHN LEFT HALF

BAKER RIGHT HALF

HAPGOOD LEFT BACK

ROBERTS CENTRE BACK

PARKER RIGHT BACK

PREEDY GOALKEEPER

THE CLASSIC OFFSIDE TRAP

One tactic that has, at different times, been synonymous with Arsenal has been the use of the offside trap. Although Arsenal could not be credited with devising the tactic itself, it was Herbert Chapman's use of a third centre back played slightly behind the full backs which gave the team the opportunity to deploy a very effective line.

Future Gunners teams continued to use the tactic, as did every other side once its advantages became obvious. However, it was probably at its most potent when George Graham put together the back four of Nigel Winterburn, Tony Adams, Steve Bould and Lee Dixon in the late 1980s. Their understanding was such that they were rarely caught out and often compressed play by keeping a high line. This, especially at free kicks, helped ease the pressure on the keeper.

David Seaman said of the 1994 Cup-Winners' Cup final, "That was the one time I really enjoyed the offside rule. We were just holding the box and every time they were running in they got caught offside." The trap played its part in the 1990/91 championship, when only 18 goals were conceded in 38 league games.

The tactic was successful so often that, in the eyes of many opposition fans, the eternal image of Tony Adams is with his arm raised appealing to the linesman for a decision. "There have been a lot of jokes about that," says Lee Dixon, "like the Arsenal Subbuteo team with the back four having their hands in the air."

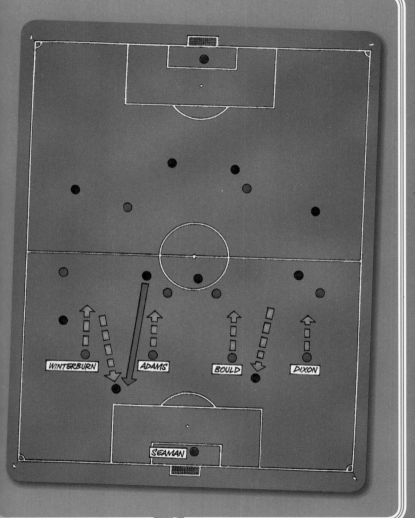

WINTERBURN ADAMS BOULD DIXON

SEAMAN

GRAHAM'S DEFENSIVE MASTERCLASS

When Arsenal reached the 1994 European Cup-Winners' Cup final against holders Parma in Copenhagen, the Italian side were clear favourites to retain the trophy, not least because the Gunners had their key men Ian Wright and John Jensen unavailable. But the team had become adept at winning big one-off matches through determined defending, and ultimately George Graham's tactics proved the difference between the sides.

He was able to field his trusted backline of Lee Dixon, Steve Bould, Tony Adams and Nigel Winterburn in front of David Seaman, with a five-man midfield in front of them. The wide players were instructed to funnel attacks into the centre, where the crowded midfield and two combative centre backs meant that, in the words of Alan Smith, Parma, "weren't allowed to play at all".

Parma may have had superior technical players in Gianfranco Zola, Faustino Asprilla and Tomas Brolin but, denied room, could not make it count. Tony Adams remembers, "We won by tangling them up in a spider's web."

It was the season that the '1-0 to the Arsenal' chant was born, and there was no better demonstration of it than this game. The Gunners only needed to score once and then rely on their men at the back. Smith scored the required goal in the 20th minute. He reflects today, "It was the pinnacle of that back four's effectiveness. Once I'd scored, it was all about them. They were just awesome that night."

The remainder of the final was a defensive masterclass. As George Graham recalled, "Once we went a goal in front I knew we had a chance because our strength was keeping clean sheets."

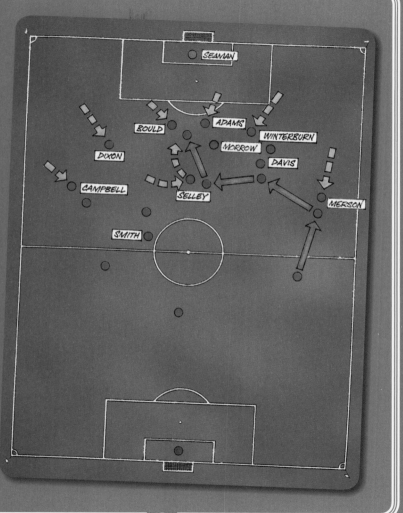

WENGER'S LIGHTNING FAST TOTAL FOOTBALL

Arsène Wenger's football philosophy is to play "a game based on technical skill, mobility, dynamism and creativity". He attempts to build teams that feature players embodying all of these traits, and when he has achieved this, Arsenal win silverware.

He recruits players he believes can express his idea of 'total football' – a concept whose origins lie in the Ajax team of the early 1970s – but Wenger adds the twist of supreme pace. The Ajax-developed Dennis Bergkamp described Arsenal's football in the team that won five major trophies between 2002 and 2005 as "the closest I have seen to the Dutch concept of total football".

Wenger's favoured qualities were encapsulated by a goal in the match at White Hart Lane that sealed the Premiership in 2004. Forward Thierry Henry carried the ball out of defence after a Tottenham corner into the opposition half. There, he read the run of Bergkamp, hugging the left wing, to the corner of the penalty area. The Dutchman took just one touch to send the ball into the path of onrushing midfielder Patrick Vieira, who had run the length of the pitch, to connect and score.

It mattered not which position the players were supposed to fill, all had licence to play with expression as and where they saw fit, and at breakneck speed if required, all the while with an almost telepathic understanding of the space their team-mates would run into. At times, they were simply unplayable. Leeds's Olivier Dacourt described playing Wenger's team as "demoralising. They just pass and move, pass and move. You find yourself working for nothing."

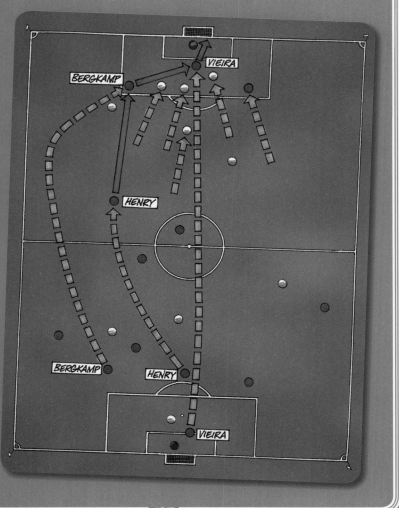

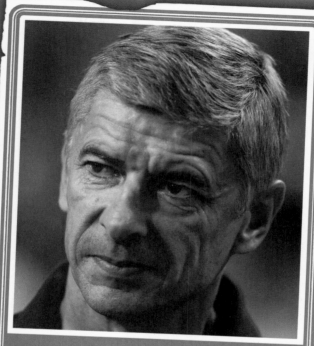

GREAT GAFFERS

Herbert Chapman was the first manager to win a major trophy for Arsenal, the 1930 FA Cup, and he transformed the club into one of the greatest names of English football history.

A visionary in all aspects of the game, Chapman ensured the fitness of his team was superior to others, at the same time as treating them with more respect than was normally afforded to footballers. In this way he did what he could to get the best from his players physically, mentally, technically and tactically.

George Allison consulted the players closely...

Arriving from reigning champions Huddersfield in 1925, he constantly looked to strengthen his side, and despite taking the club to its first FA Cup final in 1927 it was not until Chapman was given significant funds to bring in better players that Arsenal became a major force. The seven trophies won in the 1930s suggest the club could have won even more if they'd speculated to accumulate more in his early seasons at Highbury.

Chapman passed away in January 1934 due to pneumonia after watching three matches in three days, having refused to rest on developing a cold. Proof indeed of his dedication to the club and his job.

George Allison was the club's managing director and took over as manager. Chapman's assistant and future club secretary Bob Wall said that Allison, "never claimed to possess a deep theoretical knowledge of the game but he listened closely to what people like Tom Whittaker and Alex James had to say. He always insisted that he would secure a prospective signing only if his character was beyond reproach."

His purchase of key players such as Ted Drake and Wilf Copping continued his predecessor's aim of constantly improving the team and Arsenal's success did not

...a productive approach continued by his successor Tom Whittaker

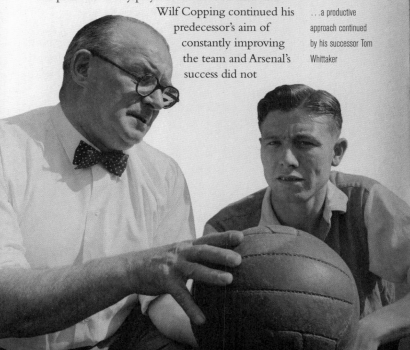

Bertie Mee's disciplinarian approach took his team to Double success

abate until the outbreak of the Second World War. But by the time football recommenced, the team needed rebuilding and Allison only managed for one more season before retiring.

He handed the reins over to physio (and former player) Tom Whittaker and the results were immediate. Arsenal regained the League Championship during his first season in charge and there followed an FA Cup and a further title in the next five years. Whittaker had a polite but effective manner with the players. Joe Mercer described him as "the greatest man I ever met". However, he was unable to match the sustained success of the 1930s as he found it difficult to attract major stars. He died of a heart attack in 1956 and the club then employed a succession of managers, all of whom failed to bring success.

That changed with the promotion of another Arsenal physio to the manager's post. Bertie Mee took over in 1966 and developed a young group of players that would eventually bring success back to the club. Mee had a military air about him and allowed no slacking, with a frequently stated purpose of "stopping mediocrity being perpetuated". He employed great coaches in Dave Sexton and Don Howe and bought necessary players astutely to build a side that peaked with the 1971 league and FA Cup 'double', something even the great team of the 1930s had failed to achieve.

Terry Neill achieved Cup success but fell out with some of his squad

Mee knew how to get the best from his players, building his side on the basis of youthful camaraderie and intense effective teamwork rather than reliance on prima donnas. However, there was criticism that his double-winning side were boring, which perhaps played a part in his allowing some squad members to leave when they could have served the club better than those who replaced them. Mee resigned in 1976 as Arsenal failed to build on their 1971 success, and the departure of Howe after the double season may well have been a key factor in this respect. Mee's replacement

The players called George Graham 'Gaddafi' and his approach dictated success

Terry Neill, in spite of building a team of talented players, only managed to land a solitary FA Cup in seven seasons.

Former player George Graham arrived from managing Millwall in 1986 and echoing the ways of Mee, whom he had served under, rebuilt the team with a mix of the youngsters on the club's books and bargain buys, some from lower divisions. His disciplinarian ways were in huge contrast to his playing days. David O'Leary later claimed that "George liked his Gaddafi reputation", a reference to the nickname the players gave him due to his dictatorial approach. If he ruled by fear, the early results were impressive, with two titles and a League Cup under his belt in his first five seasons.

However, concentration on replicating the ethos of the 1971 double team – "If you weren't working hard, you weren't playing," remembers Paul Merson – resulted in creative players becaming something of a luxury and the team's ability to win matches consistently declined. The players were still able to grind out results selectively and in the latter stages of

Graham's time three cups were won. However the 'bung' scandal in the autumn of 1994 signalled the end of his era a few months later.

Arsène Wenger's arrival in 1996 proved a breath of fresh air, as he set about transforming the reputation of Arsenal and ultimately its physical surroundings – namely state of the art training facilities and the move to a new stadium in 2006. His impact on both the club and English football proved as significant as Chapman's decades earlier, with a new, more scientific approach to the fitness and conditioning of footballers, as well as the utilisation of a far greater number of foreign imports than before his arrival.

Arsenal benefited through both trophies – seven between 1998 and 2005 – and a fabulous footballing style that resulted in invariable sell-outs, even in the new 60,000-seater stadium. As Champions League football has become financially imperative, Wenger has ensured continuous qualification for the tournament for over a decade, no mean feat considering the financial restrictions under which he has had to operate. He has secured the club's status as one of the world's elite group of superclubs, and testimony to his reputation is the constant courting by Real Madrid.

Arsène Wenger totally transformed the club, elevating it to its greatest heights

MEMORABLE
MATCHES

ARSENAL 3 ANDERLECHT 0

Inter-Cities Fairs Cup final 1970, 2nd Leg, Highbury, London, 28th April 1970

Having lost finals in the each of the previous two seasons, Arsenal were hoping it was a case of third time lucky when they qualified for the European Fairs Cup final in 1970, taking the notable scalp of the Johan Cruyff-inspired Ajax en route, alongside those of Glentoran, Sporting Lisbon, Rouen and Dinamo Bacau.

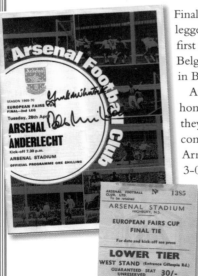

Finals in this competition were two-legged affairs at the time, and the first match against their opponents, Belgian team Anderlecht, took place in Brussels.

Arsenal were over-run by the home side – "They murdered us, if they had scored six we couldn't have complained" said winger George Armstrong – and found themselves 3-0 down after 74 minutes. An 18-year-old Ray Kennedy came on as a substitute, and scored what many felt was a consolation goal, although it later proved far more significant.

The second leg took place at Highbury two weeks later, with

Arsenal requiring a 2-0 victory to win the tie on the away goals rule. The atmosphere in the stadium that night has gone down in Arsenal legend, as a vociferous crowd willed on the team. Having been starved of a trophy

John Radford (far post) celebrates the vital second goal on a barnstorming night at Higbury

since 1953, the fans needed little motivation to give their all to encourage the players. George Armstrong described it as "the best atmosphere I've ever seen, a full house and about 40,000 outside that couldn't get in. The terraces were packed, like our 12th man." It appeared to have an effect, as Arsenal kept a clean sheet while scoring three times through Eddie Kelly, John Radford and Jon Sammels.

Anderlecht had 14 minutes to bring the scores level and force extra time, but Arsenal held firm to end the club's longest spell without a major trophy since they won their first under Herbert Chapman in 1930.

A mass pitch invasion after the presentation of the trophy saw Frank McLintock being chaired around the pitch by happy supporters. The same group of players would go on to win the league and cup double the following season, and the Fairs Cup was a vital stepping stone to that achievement.

Arsenal:
Wilson, Storey, McLintock, Simpson, McNab, Armstrong, Kelly, Sammels, Graham, Radford, George,

Scorers:
Kelly, Radford, Sammels

Attendance:
51, 612

LIVERPOOL 0 ARSENAL 2

Football League First Division, Anfield, Liverpool, 26th May 1989

After leading the 1988/89 First Division Championship for much of the season, Arsenal wobbled as they came into the final straight.

Arsenal celebrate snatching the title in an extraordinary final game at Anfield

The game against the Liverpool team chasing them had been scheduled for Sunday 23rd April, too early to be decisive. However, the Hillsborough tragedy in which many Liverpool fans lost their lives meant the fixture was rescheduled for the last Friday in May.

By this time, Liverpool's superior form meant the Gunners found themselves in second place, needing to win at Anfield by a two–goal margin to take the title they looked to have thrown away. Manager George Graham began the match by fielding a 5-3-2 formation, mindful of how important it was that his team did not concede a goal. Not needing to win, "Liverpool played into our hands," Graham remembers,

the home side content to play the game out rather than perform to their capabilities. At half time it was scoreless, although the Arsenal boss was perfectly happy as he had predicted the necessary goals would come after the interval.

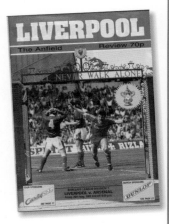

He was proved correct, as the visitors took the lead thanks to an indirect free kick after 55 minutes. Nigel Winterburn floated the ball in and striker Alan Smith made contact with the side of his head to divert the ball into the net. The Liverpool players furiously appealed the goal was illegal, but to no avail.

As injury time neared, the chances of the vital second goal looked slim, but a long ball pumped forward to Alan Smith was knocked on to midfielder Mickey Thomas, who received a lucky deflection off opposing defender Steve Nicol before regaining control and honing in on the goal. ITV commentator Brian Moore famously said, "It's up for grabs now!" as Thomas shaped to shoot, chipping the ball over diving keeper Bruce Grobbelaar just before the Liverpool defenders could catch him.

"I just waited for Bruce to make the first move, like a game of chess," recalls Thomas, "and then it was down to me." Arsenal had won the championship in the most dramatic finale the competition had ever witnessed.

Arsenal: Lukic, Dixon, Bould, (Groves), O'Leary, Adams, Winterburn, Rocastle, Thomas, Richardson, Merson (Hayes), Smith,

Scorers: Smith, Thomas

Attendance: 41,783

MANCHESTER UNITED 0 ARSENAL 1

Premiership, Old Trafford, Manchester, 14th March 1998

The 1997/98 season was Arsène Wenger's first as Arsenal manager, and in the summer before the campaign he began to shake up his squad, letting English players such as Paul Merson go while signing foreign talents including Marc Overmars and Emmanel Petit.

Initially, there seemed little improvement, with the team 13 points behind leaders Manchester United by December.

However, in the league and FA Cup, the team found their form after the New Year and put together a run of 26 unbeaten games. The match that proved decisive in their assault on the title was the visit to Old Trafford in March. At the end of the previous season, United manager Alex Ferguson had said of the Arsenal boss, "He's a novice – he should keep his opinions to Japanese football." The wait for his words to come back and haunt him did not last long.

Needing to make up ground to have any chance of overtaking United, it was a must win game for the visitors, who took the game to

their opponents accordingly. Marc Overmars caused havoc on the right side of United's defence up against rookie John Curtis, who was subbed after seven minutes of the second half. As Overmars was denied a cast iron penalty and went close three times, it seemed the Gunners were destined not to claim the necessary three points.

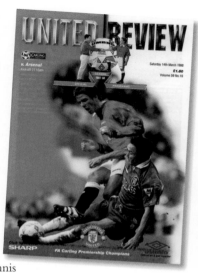

The entrance of French teenage substitute Nicolas Anelka helped to break the deadlock. In the 78th minute, a ball played up to Dennis Bergkamp was flicked on to Anelka, whose header put Overmars clear of the defence. His pace ensured he would not be caught and this time he beat keeper Peter Schmeichel from the angle. "He showed he's a big game player," Wenger said of Overmars afterwards.

The victory gave Arsenal the belief they could win the club's first title since 1991. "Why shouldn't we win the title? If we win our games in hand, we are ahead," said Overmars. The team duly won their next eight matches, making up a further six points on United, to secure the Premiership trophy with two fixtures to spare.

Arsenal:
Manninger, Dixon, Keown, Adams, Winterburn, Parlour (Garde), Vieira, Petit, Overmars, Bergkamp, Wreh (Anelka)

Scorers:
Overmars

Attendance:
55,174

REAL MADRID 0 ARSENAL 1

Champions League Round of 16, First Leg,
Estadio Santiago Bernabéu, Madrid,
21st February 2006

Under Arsène Wenger, Arsenal had enjoyed eight consecutive seasons of Champions League football, but by the quirk of the draw had never faced one particular continental giant until the 2005/06 competition. Then, in the first knockout round, they were paired with the legendary Real Madrid.

It was a tie Gooners had waited years for, the away game akin to a pilgrimage and tickets were like gold dust. Arsenal's defence had been ravaged by injuries, with three of the first choice players absent, yet the team surprised the travelling fans as they more than matched a Real side including such luminaries as Zinedine Zidane, Ronaldo, David Beckham, Raul and Roberto Carlos. In contrast to their hosts, the Gunners blended experience and youth in their line-up but there was no indication of stage fright.

Wenger's team, with five in midfield, hustled

their hosts out of their stride, surprising the locals who had expected to see the customary attacking football from the men in white. In fact it was Arsenal who did the majority of the foraying forward, as their midfield supported the lone striker consistently. "You see that as soon as Arsenal is not scared to play, we can play good football,' said captain Thierry Henry afterwards.

Thierry Henry capped a wonderful display with a fine goal

In one of his best ever performances for the club, it was he who settled the evening with a wonder goal in the 47th minute. Collecting the ball from Cesc Fabregas close to the centre circle, his pace took him past four defenders before he scored with a low shot across keeper Iker Casillas. It was one of many attempts, and Wenger's words afterwards – "My only regret is that we did not add one or two more goals" – indicated just how good Arsenal had been as they became the first English side to win at the Bernabéu.

A dramatic return leg ended goalless, and Real were eliminated, in spite of their stellar line-up. Henry's strike in Madrid proved the key moment, a huge step in a campaign that would end with Arsenal's first ever Champions League final appearance, ironically in the striker's home city of Paris.

Arsenal:
Lehmann, Eboue, Toure, Senderos, Flamini, Ljungberg, Fabregas (Song), Gilberto, Hleb (Pires), Reyes (Diaby), Henry

Scorers: Henry

Attendance: 80,000

ARSENAL COMIC STRIP HISTORY 4

SEPTEMBER 2002...ARSENE WENGER, MANAGER OF THE DEFENDING CHAMPIONS, IS GIVING A PRESS CONFERENCE...

IT WILL BE DIFFICULT FOR US TO GO THROUGH THE SEASON UNBEATEN, BUT WE CAN DO IT.

A MONTH LATER THE GUNNERS LOSE A PREMIERSHIP MATCH FOR THE FIRST TIME SINCE DECEMBER 2001...

SOON A T-SHIRT IS PRODUCED LAMPOONING WENGER IN THE STYLE OF THE IRAQI INFORMATION MINISTER KNOWN AS 'COMICAL ALI'...

BUT WENGER HAS THE LAST LAUGH WHEN, A SEASON LATER, ARSENAL WIN THE TITLE UNDEFEATED...

...AND A FAN GIVES HIM ONE OF THE SHIRTS AS THE TEAM PARADE THE TROPHY AFTER THE FINAL HOME GAME!

THE STORY OF THE GUNNERS
WENGER'S ARSENAL
1995-2010

In the 1995 close season, Arsenal unveiled the then Bolton boss Bruce Rioch as the man to succeed George Graham. He was the first Arsenal manager since Billy Wright in the 1960s without previous links to the club.

His first few weeks saw superstars Dennis Bergkamp and David Platt join from the Italian league. With such big names on board, it was expected that the team would do better than the fifth-place they achieved, but they didn't and Rioch departed. It later transpired that the next manager, Frenchman Arsène Wenger, might have been given the job earlier had some directors been less cautious about hiring a continental who lacked experience of the English game. That they had the opportunity to reverse that decision in 1996 was a major turning point in the club's history.

Having only managed in France and Japan, Arsène Wenger was almost completely unknown, with London's *Evening Standard* carrying the headline 'Arsène Who?' when news came through that he was Rioch's successor. Yet he transformed both the team and the English footballing culture whilst extending the careers of an experienced defence that had gone off the boil somewhat towards the end of George Graham's reign. He achieved this while also rebuilding both midfield and attack with imported bargains to make the club a dominant force in Premiership football.

Dennis Bergkamp, arguably the single most pivotal player in modern Arsenal history

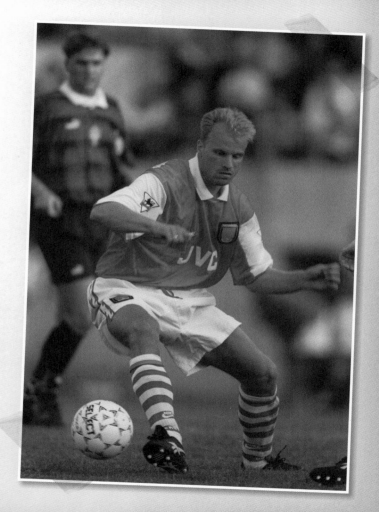

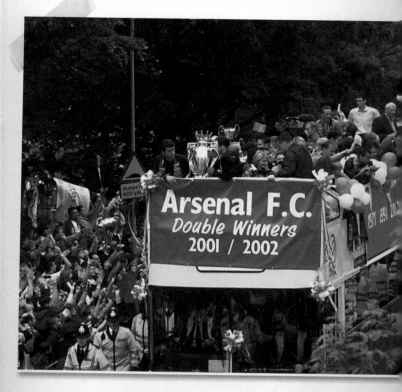

Arsenal's all-conquering men and women parade their trophy haul down Islington's Upper Street

Wenger guided the team to third place in his first season, despite arriving part way through due to his contractual commitments to Japan's Grampus Eight. In his first full campaign Arsenal won the League and FA Cup double. For the next seven seasons, the club would never finish outside the top two, an incredible

achievement given how little money the manager spent. Quite apart from having an eye for fine players that he could improve further, Wenger would often turn a significant profit when players left the club.

Among the stars from the era that proved to be bargain buys were Patrick Vieira, Marc Overmars, Emmanuel Petit, Nicolas Anelka, Thierry Henry and Robert Pires. All departed for teams in Spain or Italy and aside from Pires, who was out of contract, commanded huge fees, allowing Wenger to buy cheaper replacements.

After Wenger's first double, Arsenal remained competitive in both league and cups, but it was four years before the next trophy arrived. However, the fabulous football being played was invariably packing out the 38,500 capacity Highbury stadium, despite ever-increasing ticket prices. So the directors decided the club required a new stadium to allow more fans to see matches and increase turnover to pay for the best players. Their existing stadium could not be expanded sufficiently due to the surrounding housing, but a new site, Ashburton Grove – at the centre of which Islington's rubbish was processed – was found a few hundred metres west to allow the club to remain in the area. Having already proved a prudent operator in the transfer market, the manager would now have no choice, as the club took out huge loans to fund the building of their new home.

While the new stadium was under construction, Arsenal enjoyed a memorable four seasons in which they won the league twice (2002 and 2004) and the FA Cup three times (2002, 2003 and 2005 – all in Cardiff, as Wembley was being rebuilt). Wenger's players peaked for the 2003/04 title in which their crowning achievement was to remain unbeaten over the course of the entire league campaign. That team became known as 'The Invincibles' and with matches in the seasons before and after, put together a record total of

49 league games without defeat. It was a phenomenal achievement, not least because they continued to play attacking football that was pleasing on the eye.

In 2005/06 came the club's final season at Highbury, and fans also saw the team progress to a Champions League final against Barcelona. They were

Fans say goodbye to Highbury on 7 May 2006. That fella in the crowd looks familiar...

unfortunate to be reduced to ten men early in the game when their Spanish opponents scored, only for the referee to award a foul instead and dismiss Arsenal's keeper Jens Lehmann. Despite this, Arsenal took the lead, only to be worn down by their opponents and eventually lose 2-1. The competition that year had provided some memorable nights at Highbury, with matches against Real Madrid and Juventus giving the old stadium a fantastic send off. The last European fixture staged was a semi-final first leg against Villarreal, remembered for the famous 'Highbury squirrel' running around the pitch for several minutes as play continued.

The Highbury story had a happy ending with the very final match seeing Arsenal pip neighbours Tottenham to fourth place in the league, and the attendant financially crucial Champions League qualification. Tottenham only had to win at West Ham, but their team came down with food poisoning and were unable to achieve the required victory. It enabled Gunners' fans to see their team win the final game at the historic stadium (against Wigan) whilst celebrating the misfortunes of their local rivals on a glorious May day.

Wenger gradually let most of the Invincibles team depart over the course of three seasons as he rebuilt his side while the club moved the short distance to their new home, the 60,000 capacity Emirates Stadium. Financial restrictions began to bite as the manager had to prove even more spendthrift,

meaning a policy of buying younger, less proven players and allowing them to develop in the first team.

Despite this, they still offered hope that they could compete with their freer-spending rivals, challenging for the title in both 2008 and 2010 before falling short each time due to too many injuries. But there is light at the end of the tunnel, as the club have sailed the worst of the choppy financial waters induced by the stadium move, with matches continuing to sell out despite a lack of silverware

Supporters have had to be patient, but the reason for the move is to ensure Arsenal's future is one of guaranteed prosperity, leading to long term success as money becomes more and more influential in deciding football's prizes.

Arsenal fans will be looking to Robin van Persie to provide a cutting edge

THE BATTLE OF HIGHBURY

On 14th November 1934, a match took place at Highbury stadium that has gone down in Arsenal legend, despite being an international friendly fixture between England and recently crowned World Cup winners Italy. As England did not enter the tournament for the first time until 1950, it was labeled "the real World Cup final" in the English press, and was Italy's first match since winning the trophy in Paris. Italian Prime Minister Benito Mussolini reportedly offered each of the national team's players an Alfa Romeo car and a substantial bonus payment if they won.

Five of the seven Arsenal players who lined up for England (from left) Copping, Hapgood, Moss, Bowden, Bastin

However, what occurred could also fuel the argument that the Arsenal side of this period was the best team on the planet, as all but four of those selected to represent England were Gunners' players. They had

won two consecutive league titles and were in the process of securing a third. Seven players from one club starting an England international set a record that has not been eclipsed. They were Frank Moss, George Male, Eddie Hapgood, Wilf Copping, Ray Bowden, Ted Drake and Cliff Bastin. A young winger named Stanley Matthews won his third cap, and that none of those on duty had made ten international appearances was testimony to the inexperience of the line-up.

The game became known as The Battle of Highbury due to the violence of the encounter. Matthews later described it as the most violent game of his career, which lasted a further 30 years. It was indicative that the man of the match was hard man Copping, for his

Led by legendary manager Vittorio Pozzo (far left), the Italians line up before a training session at White Hart Lane

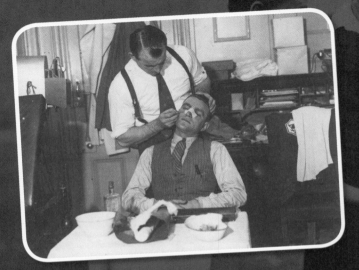

Arsenal trainer Tom Whittaker tends to Eddie Hapgood's broken nose after the bloody battle

battling display in midfield. England fittingly lined up in the 3-4-3 formation that Herbert Chapman had introduced at Arsenal, against Italy's more traditional 2-5-3. Eight of their players were drawn from two clubs – Inter and Juventus, so there was plenty of familiarity in their roster.

The nature of the contest was set from the start, with an early challenge from Ted Drake breaking the foot of opposition centre half Luis Monti. After two minutes, and decades before substitutes existed, Italy were down to ten men. They did not take kindly to losing their man to a bad tackle, and retaliated in kind. Among the injuries suffered by English players were a broken nose for Hapgood (who missed 15 minutes of the match while being treated), a damaged ankle for Bowden and a fractured arm for Manchester City striker Eric Brook. Drake was also punched. If Arsene Wenger frets about the danger of his players being injured on international duty, a history lesson might prove enlightening.

Despite the aggressive nature of the afternoon, England were focused enough to take advantage of their extra man, with two goals from Brook (after he had missed a penalty), followed up by another courtesy of Drake to give the home country a convincing lead. Italy rallied after the interval, Giuseppe Meazza scoring twice, hitting the woodwork and forcing some fine saves from Moss. England may have won 3-2, but due to their playing almost the entire match a man down, the losers were still feted back home, and are celebrated in Italian soccer folklore as The Lions of Highbury.

The game took place 20 years before the European Champions Cup was conceived. Real Madrid's reputation was built on their domination of the competition in its early days, as later those of Ajax, Real Madrid, Liverpool and AC Milan would be. The Battle of Highbury was persuasive evidence that, if it had existed in the 1930s, Arsenal would have enjoyed a similar period of domination over Europe as they had over England.

ENGLAND 3 ITALY 2

Friendly International, Highbury, London, 14th November 1934

England:
Moss, Male, Barker (Derby), Hapgood, Britton (Everton), Copping, Bowen, Bastin, Matthews (Stoke), Drake, Brook (Manchester City)

Scorers:
Brook 2, Drake

Attendance:
56,044

HONOURS AND RECORDS

MAJOR HONOURS

WINNERS

Football League Champions: 1931, 1933, 1934, 1935, 1938, 1948, 1953, 1971, 1989, 1991

Premier League Champions: 1998, 2002, 2004

FA Cup: 1930, 1936, 1950, 1971, 1979, 1993, 1998, 2002, 2003, 2005

League Cup: 1987, 1993

European Inter-Cities Fairs Cup: 1970

European Cup Winners' Cup: 1994

Charity/Community Shield: 1930, 1931, 1933, 1934, 1938, 1948, 1953, 1991 (shared), 1998, 1999, 2002, 2004

FA Youth Cup: 1966, 1971, 1988, 1994, 2000, 2001, 2009

RUNNERS-UP

Football League: 1926, 1932, 1973

Premier League: 1999, 2000, 2001, 2003, 2005

FA Cup: 1927, 1932, 1952, 1972, 1978, 1980, 2001

League Cup: 1968, 1969, 1988, 2007

UEFA Champions League: 2006

UEFA Cup: 2000

European Cup Winners' Cup: 1980, 1995

RECORDS

COMPETITION/INTERNATIONAL RECORDS

- Most consecutive seasons in English top flight: 84 (up to 2009/10)
- **Longest unbeaten sequence in English top flight: 49 matches (May 2003 - Oct 2004)**
- Longest unbeaten away sequence in English league football: 27 matches (5th April 2003 - 25th Sept 2004)
- **Most consecutive scoring league games in English domestic football: 55 (19th May 2001 - 30th Nov 2002)**
- Most consecutive scoring away games: 27 (19th May 2001 - 23rd Nov 2002)
- **Most players from one club in an England starting line-up: 7 (14th Nov 1934 v Italy)**
- Youngest player to play for England: Theo Walcott, 17 years 75 days (30th May 2006, England v Hungary)
- **Highest League attendance : 83,260 (Manchester United v Arsenal, at Maine Road, First Division, 17th Jan 1948)**
- Most consecutive league wins: 14 (Feb - Aug 2002)
- **Most consecutive away league matches unbeaten: 27 (5th April 2003 - 24th Oct 2004)**
- Fewest failures to score in a league season: 0 (Scored in every game), 2001/02
- **Most away league goals scored in a season: 60, 1930/31**
- Fastest goal by a substitute: 1.8 seconds, Nicklas Bendtner (v Tottenham Hotspur, 22nd Dec 2007)
- **Most consecutive matches in the Champions League without**

conceding a goal: 10 (18th Oct 2005-26 April 2006)

CLUB RECORDS

- Highest Home Attendance: (Highbury) 73,295 v Sunderland, 9th Mar, 1935; (Wembley) 73,707 v Lens, 25th Nov 1998; (Emirates) 60,161 v Manchester United, 3rd Nov, 2007
- **Biggest home win: 12-0 v Loughborough Town, 12th March 1900 (Division 2) & v Ashford United, 14th Oct 1893 (FA Cup)**
- Biggest away win: 7-0 v Standard Liege, 3rd Nov 1993 (European Cup Winners' Cup)
- **All competitions consecutive wins: 14 (12th Sept 1987 - 21st Nov 1987)**
- Consecutive Football League wins: 10 (12th Sept 1987 - 21st Nov 1987)
- **Consecutive Premiership wins: 14 (10th Feb 2002 - 24th Aug 2002)**
- Consecutive matches unbeaten: 28 (9th April 2007 - 24 Nov 2007)
- **Consecutive Football League matches unbeaten: 26 (28th April 1990 - 2nd Feb 1991)**
- Consecutive Premiership matches unbeaten: 49 (7th May 2003 - 1st Feb 2005)
- **Consecutive Premiership matches scoring: 55 (19th May 2001 - 7th Dec 2002)**
- Most league wins in a season: 29 in 42 matches, First Division, 1970/71
- **Most league goals scored in a season: 127 in 42 matches, First Division, 1930/31**

- Most points in a league season (2 for a win): 66 in 42 matches, First Division, 1930/31
- **Most points in a league season (3 for a win): 90 in 38 matches, Premier League, 2003/04**

INDIVIDUAL RECORDS
FOOTBALLER OF THE YEAR
1950: Joe Mercer
1971: Frank McLintock
1998: Dennis Bergkamp
2002: Robert Pires
2003, 2004, 2006: Thierry Henry

PLAYERS' PLAYER OF THE YEAR
1979: Liam Brady
1998: Dennis Bergkamp
2003, 2004: Thierry Henry

PLAYERS' YOUNG PLAYER
1987: Tony Adams
1989: Paul Merson
1999: Nicolas Anelka
2008: Cesc Fabregas

FOOTBALL LEAGUE DIVISION ONE/ PREMIER LEAGUE TOP SCORERS
1934/35: Ted Drake (42 goals)
1947/48: Ronnie Rooke (33)
1976/77: Malcolm Macdonald (25)
1988/89: Alan Smith (23)
1990/91: Alan Smith (23)
1991/92: Ian Wright (29)
2001/02: Thierry Henry (24)
2003/04: Thierry Henry (30)
2004/05: Thierry Henry (25)
2005/06: Thierry Henry (27)

CLUB INDIVIDUAL RECORDS

- Most overall appearances: 722, David O'Leary (1975 - 1993)
- **Most league appearances: 558, David O'Leary (1975 - 1993)**
- Most Premiership appearances: 333, Ray Parlour (1992 - 2004)
- **Most European appearances: 78, Thierry Henry (1999 - 2007)**
- Most Champions League appearances: 70, Thierry Henry (1999 - 2007)
- **Most consecutive appearances: 172, Tom Parker (Apr 1926 - Dec 1929)**
- Youngest Player: Cesc Fabregas (16 years 177 days, League Cup v Rotherham Utd, 28th Oct 2003)
- **Oldest Player: Jock Rutherford (41 years 159 days, v Man City, 20th March 1926)**
- Record Goalscorer: 214, Thierry Henry
- **Most League goals: 164, Thierry Henry**
- Most FA Cup goals: 26, Cliff Bastin
- **Most League Cup goals: 29, Ian Wright**
- Most European goals: 41, Thierry Henry
- **Most goals in a season (all competitions): 44, Ted Drake 1934/35 (42 League, 1 FA Cup, 1 Charity Shield)**
- Most goals in one match: 7, Ted Drake (v Aston Villa, away, 14th Dec 1935, won 7-1, League)
- **Fastest recorded goal: 20.07 seconds, Gilberto v PSV, away, 25 Sept 2002)**
- Youngest goalscorer: Cesc Fabregas, (16 years 212 days v Wolves, League Cup, 2nd Dec 2003)
- **Youngest hat-trick scorer: John Radford (17 years 315 days v Wolves, League, 2nd Jan 1965)**
- Oldest goalscorer: Jock Rutherford, 39 years 352 days v Sheffield United, League, 20th Sept 1924)
- **Most capped player while playing for the club: Thierry Henry, 81 caps for France**
- Most capped England player while playing for the club: Kenny Sansom, 77 caps

FIRSTS AND LASTS

- First match: v. Eastern Wanderers, Friendly, 11th Dec 1886 (won 6-0)
- **First match as Professionals: v Sheff United, 5th Sept 1891 (lost 0-2)**
- First League match: v Newcastle United, Second Division, 2nd Sept 1893 (drew 2-2)
- **First match in First Division: v Newcastle United, 3rd Sept 1904 (lost 3-0)**
- First overseas tour match: v Belgian XI in Brussels, 5th May 1906 (won 2-1)
- **First match at Highbury: v Leicester Fosse, Second Division, 16th Sept 1913 (won 2-1)**
- First European match: v Stævnet (Copenhagen XI), Fairs Cup, 25th September 1963 (won 7-1)
- **First match at Emirates Stadium: v Ajax Amsterdam, Friendly, 22nd July 2006 (won 2-1)**
- First trophy: London Senior Cup v St. Bartholomew's Hospital (6-0) at the Kennington Oval, 7th March 1891 (six

months before turning professional)
- **First major trophy: FA Cup v Huddersfield (2-0) at Wembley, 25th Apr 1930**
- First southern club in the Football League: Admitted to Second Division in 1893
- **First Football League meeting between London clubs: Chelsea v Arsenal at Stamford Bridge, 2nd Nov 1907**
- First time players wore numbers on their backs in a Football League match: Arsenal v Sheff Weds, 25th Aug 1928
- **First time players wore squad numbers and names on their backs in a competitive English match: Arsenal v Sheff Weds, League Cup final, Wembley, 18th April 1993**
- First hat trick on full league debut: Ian Wright, v Southampton, First Division, 28th Sept 1991
- **First club to amass £100,000 gate receipts in a season: 1934/35**
- First film to be set at a football ground: *The Arsenal Stadium Mystery*, 1939
- **First match broadcast on radio: Arsenal v Sheffield United, 27th Jan 1927, transmitted on the BBC, Charlie Buchan's goal being the first on live radio commentary**
- First live football broadcast on television anywhere: Arsenal First Team v Arsenal Reserves, 16th Sept 1937
- parts of the specially arranged match were transmitted.
- **First ever game to be shown on the BBC's *Match of the Day* highlights programme: Liverpool v Arsenal, 22 Aug 1964**
- First footballer in the world to be transferred for more than £10,000: David Jack, from Bolton to Arsenal, 1928 (£10,890)
- **First team in the 20th century to participate in three consecutive F.A. Cup finals: Arsenal (1978-1980)**
- First team to win a League Championship on Goals Scored: Arsenal 1989 (level on points with Liverpool)
- **First overseas manager to win the title in England: Arsène Wenger, 1998**
- First capped Arsenal player: Caesar Jenkyns (for Wales v Scotland, 21st Mar 1896)
- **First capped Arsenal player for England: Jimmy Ashcroft (v Ireland, 17th Feb 1906)**
- First Arsenal player to captain England: David Jack, 1930
- **First Arsenal players to play in a World Cup: Dave Bowen and Jack Kelsey (for Wales v Hungary, 8th June 1958)**
- First Arsenal players to play in a World Cup for England: Graham Rix and Kenny Sansom (v France, 16th June 1982)
- **First Arsenal players to play in a World Cup final: Emmanuel Petit and Patrick Vieira (as substitute) for France v Brazil (12th July 1998)**
- First British side to defeat Real Madrid at the Bernabéu: 1-0 (UEFA Champions League second round first leg, 21st Feb 2006)
- **First team from London to reach the Champions League final: in 2006**

159

Women's Lip

About the Editor

Roz Warren is the editor of fifteen collections of women's humour, including the classic *Women's Glib*. She reviews humour books and CDs for numerous publications, and is working on her first novel. She lives in Bala Cynwyd, Pennsylvania.

Women's Lip

Outrageous, Irreverent and Hilarious Quotations

Edited by

Roz Warren

Michael O'Mara Humour

This book is dedicated with love
to my son Thomas.

First published in the United States of America
by Sourcebooks, Inc., 1998

First published in Great Britain in 2000 by
Michael O'Mara Books Limited
9 Lion Yard, Tremadoc Road
London SW4 7NQ

A CIP catalogue record for this book
is available from the British Library

ISBN 1-85479-524-4

1 3 5 7 9 10 8 6 4 2

Designed and typeset by Martin Bristow

Printed and bound in Great Britain
by Cox & Wyman Ltd, Reading, Berks

Age

"I'd like to grow very old as slowly as possible."
— *Irene Meyer Selznick*

"The hardest years in life are those between ten and seventy."

— *Helen Hayes (at 73)*

"My mother used to say: the older you get, the better you get — unless you're a banana."

— *Rose, "The Golden Girls"*

"The secret of staying young is to live honestly, eat slowly, and lie about your age."

— *Lucille Ball*

Animals

"No animal should ever jump up on the dining-room furniture unless absolutely certain that he can hold his own in the conversation."

— *Fran Lebowitz*

Art

"If you have a burning, restless urge to write or paint, simply eat something sweet and the feeling will pass."

— *Fran Lebowitz*

"Art is spirituality in drag."

— *Jennifer Unlimited*

Breaking up

"If you love someone, set them free. If they come back, they're probably broke."

— *Rhonda Dicksion*

"I broke up with my boyfriend because he wanted to get married. I didn't want him to."

— *Rita Rudner*

Q: What do you do when your boyfriend walks out?
A: Shut the door.

— *Angela Martin*

"Some people have their marriages annulled, which means they never existed. Boy, talk about denial! What do you say when people see your wedding album? 'Oh that was just some play I was in.'"

— *Carol Leifer*

Breasts

"A lot of guys think the larger a woman's breasts are, the less intelligent she is. I don't think it works like that. I think it's the opposite. I think the larger a woman's breasts are, the less intelligent the men become."

— *Anita Wise*

"Who ever thought up the word 'Mammogram'? Every time I hear it, I think I'm supposed to put my breast in an envelope and send it to someone."

— *Jan King*

Cars

"A car is just a moving, giant handbag! You never have to actually carry groceries, or dry cleaning, or anything! You can have five pairs of shoes with you at all times!"

— *Cynthia Heimel*

Cats

"Even my cat's depressed lately — I had the
exterminators in and they killed all his toys."
— *Anita Wise*

"Cats think about three things: food, sex, and nothing."
— *Adair Lara*

"I wonder what goes through his mind when he
sees us peeing in his water bowl."
— *Penny Ward Moser*

"I found out why cats drink out of the toilet.
My mother told me it's because it's cold in there.
And I'm like: 'How did my mother know that?'"
— *Wendy Liebman*

"Dogs come when they're called. Cats take a
message and get back to you."
— *Mary Bly*

"By and large, people who enjoy teaching animals to roll over will find themselves happier with a dog."

— *Barbara Holland*

"Kittens have different nutritional needs than adult cats. Consult with your veterinarian and then, for the good of your relationship with your cat, forget everything she tells you."

— *Nicole Hollander*

"I'm used to dogs. When you leave them in the morning, they stick their nose in the door crack and stand there like a portrait until you turn the key eight hours later. A cat would never put up with that kind of rejection. When you returned, she'd stalk you until you dozed off and then suck the air out of your body."

— *Erma Bombeck*

"When my cats aren't happy, I'm not happy. Not because I care about their mood but because I know they're just sitting there thinking up ways to get even."

— *Penny Ward Moser*

"Your cat will never threaten your popularity by barking at three in the morning. He won't attack the mailman or eat the drapes, although he may climb the drapes to see how the room looks from the ceiling."

— *Helen Powers*

Celebrity

"I was the toast of two continents: Greenland and Australia."

— *Dorothy Parker*

"I never made *Who's Who* but I'm featured in *What's That*."

— *Phyllis Diller*

"I stopped believing in Santa Claus at an early age. Mother took me in to see him in a department store and he asked me for my autograph."

— *Shirley Temple Black*

On Camille Paglia: "The 'g' is silent – the only thing about her that is."

– Julie Burchill

"I'm not offended by all the dumb-blonde jokes because I know that I'm not dumb. I also know I'm not blonde."

– Dolly Parton

Celibacy

"No sex is better than bad sex."

– Germaine Greer

"It's been so long since I made love, I can't even remember who gets tied up."

– Joan Rivers

"If they can put a man on the moon why can't they put one in me?"

– Flash Rosenberg

"I've reached that point in life where you have to choose between happiness and getting laid. I'm happy."

— *Mary Frances Connelly*

"To me, 'sexual freedom' means freedom from having to have sex."

— *Lily Tomlin*

Childbirth

"I realize why women die in childbirth – it's preferable."

— *Sherry Glaser*

"Dr. Simpson's first patient, a doctor's wife in 1847, had been so carried away with enthusiasm that she christened her child, a girl, 'Anaesthesia'."

— *Lady Elizabeth Longford*

Children

"A man finds out what is meant by spitting image when he tries to feed cereal to his infant."
— *Imogene Fey*

"Never allow your child to call you by your first name. He hasn't known you long enough."
— *Fran Lebowitz*

"Kids are like husbands – they're fine as long as they're someone else's."
— *Marsha Warfield*

"I met this guy who said he loved children, then I found out he was on parole for it."
— *Monica Piper*

"Boys will be noise."

— *Nina Malkin*

"My mom used to say it doesn't matter how many kids you have . . . because one kid'll take up 100% of your time so more kids can't possibly take up more than 100% of your time."

— *Karen Brown*

"Last night I was at this dinner party and my girl-friend pointed this guy out to me and said, 'Check him out — he just got divorced. He's available.' As soon as dinner was over, this guy walked over to me. He didn't know my name. He didn't know anything about me. But he said he'd been watching me and that he loved me. And that he wanted me to have his child. And he gave me his child."

— *Karen Haber*

"Little girls are cute and small only to adults. To one another they are not cute. They are life-sized."

— *Margaret Atwood*

"I want to have children while my parents are still young enough to take care of them."

— *Rita Rudner*

"Children ask better questions than adults. 'May I have a cookie?' 'Why is the sky blue?' and 'What does a cow say?' are far more likely to elicit a cheerful response than 'Where's your manuscript?' 'Why haven't you called?' and 'Who's your lawyer?'"

— *Fran Lebowitz*

"Ask your child what he wants for dinner only if he's buying."

— *Fran Lebowitz*

Christmas

"I have to admit I like Christmas cards – even though they are technically only junk mail from people you know."

— *Patricia Marx*

Coffee

"I believe humans get a lot done, not because we're smart, but because we have thumbs so we can make coffee."

— *Flash Rosenberg*

"The only thing better than Great Sex . . . is Great Coffee!"

— *Stephanie Piro*

"Never drink black coffee at lunch. It will keep you awake in the afternoon."

— *Jilly Cooper*

"Behind every successful woman . . . is a substantial amount of coffee."

— *Stephanie Piro*

Communication

"The only thing I ever said to my parents when I was a teenager was 'Hang up, I got it!'"

— *Carol Leifer*

Complaints

"I personally believe we developed language because of our deep inner need to complain."

— *Jane Wagner*

"I have a 'carpe diem' mug and, truthfully, at six in the morning the words do not make me want to seize the day. They make me want to slap a dead poet."

— *Joanne Sherman*

Contraception

"For a single woman, the most effective method of oral contraception is to just yell out, 'Yes, yes, I want to have your baby!'"

— *Marsha Doble*

"I'm Catholic. My mother and I were unpacking and she found my diaphragm. I had to tell her it was a bathing cap for my cat."

— *Lizz Winstead*

"I was on stage last night and I said, 'You know the diaphragm is a pain in the ass.' Someone yelled out, 'You're putting it in the wrong place.'"

— *Carole Montgomery*

"A friend of mine confused her valium with her birth control pills – she had 14 kids but she didn't give a shit."

— *Joan Rivers*

Cosmetic surgery

"They can take the fat from your rear and use it to bang out dents in your face. Now that's what I call recycling. It gives a whole new meaning to dancing cheek to cheek."

— *Anita Wise*

"A forty-five-year-old woman who has had a face lift doesn't look twenty-five. If it works, she looks like a well-rested forty-three-year-old woman. If it doesn't work, she looks like a Halloween costume."

— *Fran Lebowitz*

"The thought of surgery to suck fat out of my body makes me feel sick. I could never do it. Instead of Liposuction, why not go directly to the source? I'd rather have Fridge-o-suction. Please. Instead of needless surgery just suck the food right out of my refrigerator before it even lands on me."

— *Flash Rosenberg*

"I don't plan to grow old gracefully. I plan to have face-lifts till my ears meet."

— *Rita Rudner*

"If losing your head is a be-heading, is liposuction a be-hinding?"

— *Flash Rosenberg*

Crime

"I didn't steal this. It was 'differently acquired'."
— *Sara Cytron*

Cynicism

"No matter how cynical you get, it's impossible to keep up."

— *Lily Tomlin*

"Today is the first day of the wreck of your life."
— *Becky Burke*

"Things are going to get a lot worse before they get worse."

— *Lily Tomlin*

Dating

"I live in Ithaca, a small town that seems oh-so-much-smaller when I realize that most of the single males are under twenty-two. Not that I mind the age difference, but I have this silly rule – I won't fool around with someone I could have given birth to."

— *Maxine Wilkie*

"When I was seventeen years old I was going out with a fifty-nine-year-old man. Sexually, we got along great because the things he couldn't do anymore were the things I didn't know about."

— *Carol Henry*

"My grandmother's ninety. She's dating. He's ninety-three. It's going great. They never argue. They can't hear each other."

— *Cathy Ladman*

"I don't understand when people say a lover is 'too old' or 'too young'. As far as I'm concerned, anyone who is on the planet the same time you are is fair game."

— *Flash Rosenberg*

"I went out with a guy who told me he didn't like women who were sensitive or vulnerable . . . so I stabbed him."

— *Karen Rontowski*

"I once dated a guy who was so dumb he couldn't count to twenty-one unless he was naked."

— *Joan Rivers*

"Boys don't make passes at female smart asses."

— *Letty Cottin Pogrebin*

"How many of you ever started dating someone because you were too lazy to commit suicide?"
— *Judy Tenuta*

"I've figured out why first dates don't work any better than they do. It's because they take place in restaurants. Women are weird and confused and unhappy about food, and men are weird and confused and unhappy about money, yet off they go, the minute they meet, to where you use money to buy food."
— *Adair Lara*

"This guy says, 'I'm perfect for you, 'cause I'm a cross between a macho and a sensitive man.' I said, 'Oh, a gay trucker?'"
— *Judy Tenuta*

Death

"*Final Exit*, the suicide how-to book, was a best-seller for 19 weeks after its publication. One year later, the paperback version came out and did a brisk business. Our questions: Who waited for the paperback? And what did the self-destructive cheapskates do with their savings?"
— 101 Reasons Why We're Doomed
by Meredith Anthony & Alison Power

"The dying process begins the minute we are born, but it accelerates during dinner parties."
— *Carol Matthau*

"We're all cremated equal."
— *Jane Ace*

"They say you shouldn't say nothing about the dead unless it's good. He's dead. Good."
— *Moms Mabley*

Dentists

"I ran into my dentist. At first I didn't know it was him. But then I looked up his nose."

— *Judy Tenuta*

Dieting

"I've been on a constant diet for the last two decades. I've lost a total of 789 pounds. By all accounts, I should be hanging from a charm bracelet."

— *Erma Bombeck*

"The only way to lose weight is to check it in as airline baggage."

— *Peggy Ryan*

"I bought a talking refrigerator that said 'Oink' every time I opened the door. It made me hungry for pork chops."

— *Marie Mott*

"Food is like sex: when you abstain, even the worst stuff begins to look good."

— *Beth McCollister*

"A great many people in Los Angeles are on strict diets that restrict their intake of synthetic foods. The reason for this appears to be a widely-held belief that organically grown fruit and vegetables make the cocaine work faster."

— *Fran Lebowitz*

"I got so depressed about dieting that I had to see a doctor. He said, 'For God's sake, pull yourself together.' He was trying to get me through the door."

— *Florence Small*

"A waist is a terrible thing to mind."

— *Jane Caminos*

"I've decided that perhaps I'm bulimic and just keep forgetting to purge."

— *Paula Poundstone*

Divorce

"There is so little difference between husbands, you might as well keep the first."
— *Adela Rogers St. Johns*

"I never even believed in divorce until after I got married."
— *Diane Ford*

"The wages of sin is alimony."
— *Caryoln Wells*

"When I'm dating I look at a guy and wonder, 'Is this the man I want my children to spend their weekends with?'"
— *Rita Rudner*

Doctors

"A male gynaecologist is like an auto mechanic who never owned a car."

— *Carrie Snow*

"Dermatologists make rash judgments."

— *Patricia Majewski*

Dogs

"Pugs are living proof that God has a sense of humour."

— *Margo Kaufman*

Drinking

"One more drink and I'll be under the host."

— *Dorothy Parker*

"I've been SOBER a while. To me, SOBER stands for 'Son-of-a-Bitch, Everything's Real!'"

— *Kathy G*

"I don't drink or do any drugs. I never have and I never will. I don't need them. I'm a Black woman from the land of the free, home of the brave and I figure I don't need another illusion."

— *Bertice Berry*

"Alcoholism isn't a spectator sport. Eventually the whole family gets to play."

— *Joyce Rebeta-Burditt*

"They're trying to put warning labels on liquor. 'Caution: Alcohol can be dangerous to pregnant women.' That's ironic. If it weren't for alcohol, most women wouldn't even be that way."

— *Rita Rudner*

Driving

"Naples traffic isn't a condition. It's a war in progress."

— *Erma Bombeck*

"My licence plate says PMS. Nobody cuts me off."
— *Wendy Liebman*

Education

"I read Shakespeare and the Bible and I can shoot dice. That's what I call a liberal education."

— *Tallulah Bankhead*

Ego

"It takes a lot of time to be a genius — you have to sit around so much doing nothing, really nothing."
— *Gertrude Stein*

"Listen, everyone is entitled to my opinion."

> — *Madonna*

"Egotism — usually just a case of mistaken nonentity."

> — *Barbara Stanwyck*

"Success didn't spoil me; I've always been insufferable."

> — *Fran Lebowitz*

"He was the most self-involved guy I ever met in my life. He had a coffee mug on his table that said, 'I'm the greatest.' He had a plaque on the wall that said, 'I'm number one.' And on his bedspread it said, 'The Best.' In the middle of making love he said, 'Move over — you're getting in my way.'"

> — *Karen Haber*

Environment

"The other day I bought a wastebasket and carried it home in a paper bag. And when I got home I put the paper bag in the wastebasket."

— *Lily Tomlin*

Exercise

"They kept telling us we had to get in touch with our bodies. Mine isn't all that communicative but I heard from it on Tuesday morning when I genially proposed, 'Body, how'd you like to go to the nine o'clock class in vigorous toning with resistance?' Clear as a bell my body said, 'Listen, bitch, do it and you die.'"

— *Molly Ivins*

"I've been doing leg lifts faithfully for about fifteen years, and the only thing that has gotten thinner is the carpet where I have been doing the leg lifts."

— *Rita Rudner*

"I have to exercise in the morning before my brain figures out what I'm doing."

— *Marsha Doble*

"I don't think jogging is healthy, especially morning jogging. If morning joggers knew how tempting they looked to morning motorists, they would stay home and do sit-ups."

— *Rita Rudner*

"My grandmother started walking five miles a day when she was sixty. She's ninety-three today and we don't know where the hell she is."

— *Ellen Degeneres*

Experience

"I'm an experienced woman; I've been around . . . Well, all right, I might not've been around, but I've been . . . nearby."

— *Mary Richards, 'Mary Tyler Moore Show'*

"When women go wrong, men go around after them."

— *Mae West*

"A girl can wait for the right man to come along but in the meantime that still doesn't mean she can't have a wonderful time with all the wrong ones."

— *Cher*

"My heart is as pure as the driven slush."

— *Tallulah Bankhead*

"To err is human but it feels divine."

— *Mae West*

"Keep a diary and one day it'll keep you."

— *Mae West*

Family

"It looks like the 'don't ask—don't tell' policy will go into effect . . . which, I believe, is the creed of dysfunctional families everywhere."
— *Beverly Mickins*

On her proposed Academy Award acceptance speech: "I'd like to thank my mother and my father for providing me with the need to seek the love of strangers."
— *Betsy Salkind*

"I've been talking about my family with my therapist for so long that by now she has her own problems with these people. Last week, when I was talking about my mother, she said, 'Look, I don't want to hear a thing that woman has to say!'"
— *Sara Cytron*

"My grandmother was a very tough woman. She buried three husbands. Two of them were just napping."
— *Rita Rudner*

Fashion

"Remember that always dressing in understated good taste is the same as playing dead."
— *Susan Catherine*

"I put on a peekaboo blouse, he peeked and booed."
— *Phyllis Diller*

"It is interesting to speculate how it developed that in two of the most anti-feminist institutions, the church and the law court, the men are wearing dresses."
— *Flo Kennedy*

"I do not believe in God. I believe in cashmere."
— *Fran Lebowitz*

"If you are all wrapped up in yourself, you are overdressed."
— *Kate Halverson*

"Although a life-long fashion dropout, I have absorbed enough by reading *Harper's Bazaar* while waiting at the dentist's to have grasped that the purpose of fashion is to make A Statement. My own modest Statement, discerned by true cognoscenti, is, 'Woman Who Wears Clothes So She Won't Be Naked'."

— *Molly Ivins*

"Why is it considered seductive for women to wear beautiful clothes? Wouldn't it make more sense to wear something so ugly that a guy couldn't wait to take it off you?"

— *Flash Rosenberg*

"It's my least favourite season of the year . . . bathing suit season. I don't know why we can't all be shaped like those eighteen-year-old boys they design those suits for."

— *Diane Ford*

When a waiter at Buckingham Palace spilled soup on her dress: "Never darken my Dior again!"

— *Beatrice Lillie*

"If men can run the world, why can't they stop wearing neckties? How intelligent is it to start the day by tying a little noose around your neck?"

— *Linda Ellerbee*

"Fashion tells us that women's bodies are not supposed to be shaped like women's bodies, except during sex."

— *Julia Willis*

Q: Is lesbian dating an oxymoron?
A: No, but lesbian fashion is!

— *Lea Delaria*

"My sister has a social conscience now. She still wears her fur coat, but across the back she's embroidered a sampler that says 'Rest in Peace'."

— *Julia Willis*

"Your right to wear a mint-green polyester leisure suit ends where it meets my eye."

— *Fran Lebowitz*

"It costs a lot of money to look this cheap."
— *Dolly Parton*

"It's not true I had nothing on. I had the radio on."
— *Marilyn Monroe*

"I miss the good old days when guys wore open shirts, gold chains and polyester suits. I met many men I was attracted to. Okay so it was static cling."
— *Karen Silver*

"Now they're advertising breathable panty liners. You know some man invented that product. No woman would be inventing a panty liner and putting little holes in there. She'd put little tongues in there."

— *Diane Ford*

"Is it okay to hate men but dress just like them?"
— *Karen Ripley*

"A child develops individuality long before he develops taste. I have seen my kid straggle into the kitchen in the morning with outfits that need only one accessory: an empty gin bottle."

— *Erma Bombeck*

Fear

"Considering how dangerous everything is, nothing is frightening."

— *Gertrude Stein*

Feminism

"If you're not a feminist, you're a masochist."

— *Gloria Steinem*

Food

Q: What's an Irish Jewish seven-course meal?
A: A latke and a sixpack.

— *Caryn Leschen*

"I tried Flintstones vitamins. I didn't feel any better but I could stop the car with my feet."

— *Joan St. Onge*

"Order me anything out of season."

— *Fannie Brice*

"I try to fill the emptiness deep inside me with Cheetos, but I am still depressed. Only now my fingers are stained orange. I am blue. And I am orange."

— *Karen Salmansohn*

"Food is an important part of a balanced diet."

— *Fran Lebowitz*

"Seize the moment. Remember all those women on the *Titanic* who waved off the dessert cart."

— *Erma Bombeck*

"You've buttered your bread, now sleep in it."

— *Gracie Allen*

"I'm a Jewish girl who was raised in a vegetarian family. My dream is to open a restaurant called 'Soy Vey'."

— *Margo Black*

"This recipe is certainly silly. It says to separate two eggs, but it doesn't say how far to separate them."

— *Gracie Allen*

"When I buy cookies I just eat four and throw the rest away. But first I spray them with Raid so I won't dig them out of the garbage later. Be careful, though, because that Raid really doesn't taste that bad."

— *Janette Barber*

"Forget the withered rose or faded vow from Mr. Right. Love departs – but sauerkraut, once savoured, stays the night."

— *Barbara J. Petoskey*

"It's so beautifully arranged on the plate – you know someone's fingers have been all over it."

— *Julia Childs*

"I had left home (like all Jewish girls) in order to eat pork and take birth control pills. When I first shared an intimate evening with my husband, I was swept away by the passion (so dormant inside myself) of a long and tortured existence. The physical cravings I had tried so hard to deny, finally and ultimately sated. . . . But enough about the pork."

— *Roseanne*

Friendship

"A friend is someone you don't have to talk to anymore once the food is on the table."

— *Sabrina Matthews*

"When I was a girl I had only two friends, and they were imaginary. And they would only play with each other."

— *Rita Rudner*

Q: What can you give a friend who has everything?
A: Shelves

— *Patty Marx*

"Laugh and the world laughs with you. Cry and you cry with your girlfriends."

— *Laurie Kuslansky*

Fun

"Instant gratification takes too long."

— *Carrie Fisher*

"A desire to have all the fun is nine-tenths of the law of chivalry."

— *Dorothy Sayers*

"If only we'd stop trying to be happy we could have a pretty good time."

— *Edith Wharton*

"Too much of a good thing can be wonderful."

— *Mae West*

Games

"It's not whether you win or lose – it's how you lay the blame."

— *Fran Lebowitz*

"I figure you have the same chance of winning the lottery whether you play or not."

— *Fran Lebowitz*

Gardening

"Perennials are the ones that grow like weeds,
biennials are the ones that die this year instead of
next, and hardy annuals are the ones that never
come up at all."

— *Katharine Whitehorn*

Gossip

"If you can't say anything good about someone, sit
right here by me."

— *Alice Roosevelt Longsworth*

"I hate to spread rumours — but what else can one
do with them?"

— *Amanda Lear*

Gynaecology

"I got a postcard from my gynaecologist. It said 'Did you know it's time for your annual check-up?' No, but now my mailman does."

– *Cathy Ladman*

Hair

"I've been in this hair change mode for several years – it grows from a fear that I will end up like Margaret Mead or Mamie Eisenhower and adopt a style in my twenties, stick with it no matter what, and look like a clown with a danish on my head at seventy."

– *Maxine Wilkie*

"I happen to have weird hair which is why I don't dress up fancy. If I dress up, people just look at me and go, 'Oooh, look at her head.' This way here, it's more of a total look and nobody can put their finger on quite what they think is wrong."

– *Paula Poundstone*

"Guys are lucky because they get to grow moustaches. I wish I could. It's like having a little pet for your face."

— *Anita Wise*

"I refuse to think of them as chin hairs. I think of them as stray eyebrows."

— *Janette Barber*

"I'm worried that my hair is going to get bigger than I am and take me places I don't want to go."

— *Jennifer Heath*

"The heck with the natural look. After all, you can't take credit for what you're born with, only for what you do yourself. Where would Marilyn Monroe be if she'd clung to the hair colour God gave her? We'd have a movie called *Gentlemen Prefer Mousy Brown Hair*."

— *Adair Lara*

Health

"Health – what my friends are always drinking to before they fall down."

— *Phyllis Diller*

"Never go to a doctor whose office plants have died."

— *Erma Bombeck*

"Happiness is good health and a bad memory."

— *Ingrid Bergman*

"Life is drab unless we make the most of each new experience. Should sickness be an exception? If you want to live life to the fullest, why not glorify each symptom and dramatize each twinge? Don't just sit there – worry about your health."

— *Carol L. King*

Hell

"My idea of hell is to be stranded on a desert island with nothing to read but Anaïs Nin's diaries."
                                        — *Katha Pollitt*

"In hell all the messages you ever left on answering machines will be played back to you."
                                        — *Judy Horacek*

Home

"Home is a great place — after all the other places have closed."
                                        — *Texas Guinan*

Housekeeping

"I'm a wonderful housekeeper. Every time I get divorced, I keep the house."
                                        — *Zsa Zsa Gabor*

"My second favourite household chore is ironing.
My first being hitting my head on the top bunk bed
until I faint."

— *Erma Bombeck*

"A dish that don't survive the dishwasher don't
deserve to live."

— *Liz Scott*

"I don't buy temporary insanity as a murder
defence. Breaking into someone's home and ironing
all their clothes is temporary insanity."

— *Sue Kolinsky*

"Nature abhors a vacuum. And so do I."

— *Anne Gibbons*

"I prefer the word homemaker, because housewife
always implies that there may be a wife someplace
else."

— *Bella Abzug*

"I would rather lie on a sofa than sweep beneath it."
— *Shirley Conran*

"If you want to get rid of stinking odours in the kitchen, stop cooking."
— *Erma Bombeck*

"Don't cook. Don't clean. No man will ever make love to a woman because she waxed the linoleum – 'My God, the floor's immaculate. Lie down, you hot bitch.'"
— *Joan Rivers*

"I know people who are so clean you can eat off their floors. You can't eat off my table. Fang, my husband, says the only thing domestic about me is that I was born in this country."
— *Phyllis Diller*

Hunters

"I ask people why they have deer heads on their walls. They always say, 'Because it's such a beautiful animal.' There you go! I think my mother is attractive, but I have photographs of her."
— *Ellen Degeneres*

Illness

"I'm starting to worry more about getting Alzheimer's than AIDS . . . but for the life of me, I can't remember why."
— *Anita Milner*

Inner children

"I've been having kind of a difficult day . . . my Inner Child threw up on my Higher Power."
— *Lynn Lavner*

Inner peace

"There is no such thing as inner peace. There is only nervousness and death."

— *Fran Lebowitz*

Insults

"You remind me of my brother Bosco – only he had a human head."

— *Judy Tenuta*

"Who lit the fuse on your tampon?"

— *Button*

About another actress: "She's the original good time that was had by all."

— *Bette Davis*

Jewellery

"My husband gave me a necklace. It's fake. I requested fake. Maybe I'm paranoid, but in this day and age, I don't want something around my neck that's worth more than my head."

— *Rita Rudner*

Journalism

"Journalism is the ability to meet the challenge of filling space."

— *Rebecca West*

"You should always believe all you read in the newspapers, as this makes them more interesting."

— *Rose Macaulay*

Justice

"No good deed goes unpunished."
— *Clare Boothe Luce*

"Juries scare me. I don't want to put my fate in the hands of twelve people who weren't even smart enough to get out of jury duty."
— *Monica Piper*

Laughter

"Laugh and the world laughs with you; cry and the world laughs at you."
— *Caryn Leschen*

"Laugh and the world laughs with you. Stub your toe and the world laughs whether you do or not."
— Linda Perret's Humor Files

"It's no laughing matter, but it doesn't matter if you laugh."

— *Jennie Gudmundsen*

Lawyers

"My father was a criminal lawyer. There are some people who will tell you that's redundant."

— *Lynn Lavner*

"I don't believe man is woman's natural enemy. Perhaps his lawyer is."

— *Shana Alexander*

Lesbians and gays

"The Bible contains six admonishments to homosexuals and 362 admonishments to heterosexuals. That doesn't mean that God doesn't love heterosexuals. It's just that they need more supervision."

— *Lynn Lavner*

"If we wanted to be part of an institution that is hostile to gays and women, we'd just stay home with our families."

— *Georgia Ragsdale*

"Remember the TV coverage of the Gulf War? CNN kept showing the one straight woman over there. Every hour on the hour, they'd haul her out and they'd say, 'This is Captain Mary Smith and she wants to say "hi" to her husband, Mark, and her son, Johnny.' Meanwhile, there's two thousand dykes standing behind her saying, 'Hey, Marge, keep my bowling ball polished, OK?' "

— *Robin Tyler*

"My lesbianism is an act of Christian charity. All those women out there are praying for a man, and I'm giving them my share."

— *Rita Mae Brown*

"I'm a little bit femme and a little bit butch. I wear make up . . . but I keep it in a tackle box."

— *Lynda Montgomery*

Q: How do people get to be homosexual?
A: Homosexuals are chosen first on talent, then interview, and then the swimsuit and evening gown competitions . . .

— *Suzanne Westenhoefer*

"I'm out to everybody in my family, except my aunt. She's agoraphobic, and I figure if she won't come out for me, why should I come out for her?"

— *Lynda Montgomery*

"If male homosexuals are called 'gay', then female homosexuals should be called 'ecstatic'."

— *Shelly Roberts*

"Parents should be reminded, gently and often, that, 'I love you anyway,' is not a compliment."

— *Shelly Roberts*

"I wear a T-shirt that says 'The family tree stops here'."

— *Suzanne Westenhoefer*

"When the family first comes to visit, what I did was 'de-dyke' the apartment. We call it 'straightening up'."
— *Kate Clinton*

"I'm out, therefore I am."

— *Ursula Roma*

Q: What do homosexuals do in bed?
A: It's a lot like heterosexual sex, only one of us doesn't have to fake orgasm.
— *Suzanne Westenhoefer*

"A lesbian is any uppity woman, regardless of sexual preference. If they don't call you a lesbian, you're probably not accomplishing anything."
— *Cheris Kramarae & Paula Treichler*

"I can close my eyes and still hear my mother's voice saying, 'Always remember, it's just as easy to fall in love with a rich girl as with a poor one.' Of course, she was talking to my brother at the time."
— *Lynn Lavner*

Life

"Life is short, but it's wide."

— *Jennifer Unlimited*

"Most of us live our lives devoid of cinematic moments."

— *Nora Ephron*

"Your life story would not make a good book. Don't even try."

— *Fran Lebowitz*

"Life's a bitch and then they call you one."
— *Mary Frances Connelly*

"Anybody who thinks they know everything ain't been around long enough to know anything."
— *Gladiola Montana*

"I try to take one day at a time, but sometimes several days attack me at once."

— *Jennifer Unlimited*

"Life is like a cow pasture. If you walk through it with your head down, you'll avoid the crap but never find the gate."

— The Lesbitarian

"Inside every older person is a younger person wondering what happened."

— *Jennifer Unlimited*

"I've always said that I wanted to find myself before somebody bigger did."

— *Carrie Fisher*

"I haven't known what to do for so long, I'm getting good at it."

— *Flash Rosenberg*

"Life is something to do when you can't get to sleep."

— *Fran Lebowitz*

"If I had to live my life again, I'd make all the same mistakes – only sooner."

— *Tallulah Bankhead*

"They say the movies should be more like life. I think life should be more like the movies."

— *Myrna Loy*

"It is not true that life is one damn thing after another – it's one damn thing over and over."

— *Edna St. Vincent Millay*

"If you can't be a good example, then you'll just have to be a horrible warning."

— *Catherine Aird*

Literature

"Everywhere I go I'm asked if I think universities stifle writers. My opinion is that they don't stifle enough of them."

— *Flannery O'Connor*

"I think Philip Roth is a great writer. But I wouldn't want to shake his hand."

— *Jacqueline Susann*

"The difference between owning a book and borrowing a book is that when you own it you can get food on it."

— *Susan Catherine*

"I have only read one book in my life, and that is *White Fang*. It's so frightfully good I've never bothered to read another."

— *Nancy Mitford*

"This is not a novel to be tossed lightly aside. It should be thrown with great force."

— *Dorothy Parker*

Love

"Be wary of puppy love; it can lead to a dog's life."

— *Gladiola Montana*

"'I love you' is not a question."

— *Shelly Roberts*

"Love conquers all things except poverty and a toothache."

— *Mae West*

"If love is the answer, could you please rephrase the question?"

— *Lily Tomlin*

Manners

"Familiarity doesn't breed contempt; it is contempt."
— *Florence King*

"It's all right for a perfect stranger to kiss your hand as long as he's perfect."

— *Mae West*

Make-up

"Make-up is such a weird concept, but I buy into it like every woman I know. I'll wake up in the morning and look in the mirror: 'Gee, I really don't look so good. Maybe if my eyelids were blue, I'd be more attractive. . . .'"

— *Cathy Ladman*

Marriage

"After a few years of marriage a man can look right at a woman without seeing her and a woman can see right through a man without looking at him."
— *Helen Rowland*

"In August, my husband and I celebrated our 38th wedding anniversary. You know what I finally realized? If I had killed that man the first time I thought about it, I'd have been out of jail by now."
— *Anita Milner*

"Before accepting a marriage proposal, take a good look at his father. If he's still handsome, witty, and has all his teeth . . . marry him instead."
— *Diane Jordan*

"Marrying a man is like buying something you've been admiring for a long time in a shop window. You may love it when you get it home, but it doesn't always go with everything else."
— *Jean Kerr*

"I married beneath me – all women do."

— *Nancy Astor*

"Bigamy is having one husband too many. Monogamy is the same."

— *Erica Jong*

"The surest way to be alone is to get married."

— *Gloria Steinem*

"The only thing that keeps me from being happily married . . . is my husband."

— *Andra Douglas*

"Getting married is a lot like getting into a tub of hot water. After you get used to it, it ain't so hot."

— *Minnie Pearl*

"Marriage is a souvenir of love."

— *Helen Rowland*

"It's ridiculous to think you can spend your entire life with just one person. Three is about the right number."

— *Clare Boothe Luce*

"I've married a few people I shouldn't have, but haven't we all?"

— *Mamie Van Doren*

"Any woman who still thinks marriage is a fifty-fifty proposition is only proving that she doesn't understand either men or percentages."

— *Flo Kennedy*

"The trouble with some women is that they get all excited about nothing – and then marry him."

— *Cher*

"A wedding is just like a funeral except that you get to smell your own flowers."

— *Grace Hansen*

"Marriage is a great institution, but I'm not ready for an institution yet."

— *Mae West*

"The old theory was 'Marry an older man, because they're more mature.' But the new theory is: 'Men don't mature. Marry a younger one.'"

— *Rita Rudner*

"Some of us are becoming the men we wanted to marry."

— *Gloria Steinem*

"A man in love is incomplete until he's married – then he's finished."

— *Zsa Zsa Gabor*

To George Burns: "George, you're too old to get married again. Not only can't you cut the mustard, honey, you're too old to open the jar."

— *La Wanda Page*

"I haven't known any open marriages, although quite a few have been ajar."

— *Zsa Zsa Gabor*

"Trust your husband, adore your husband, and get as much as you can in your own name."

— *Joan Rivers*

When asked why she had never married: "I can't mate in captivity."

— *Gloria Steinem*

"A girl must marry for love, and keep on marrying until she finds it."

— *Zsa Zsa Gabor*

"I'm 33, single . . . Don't you think it's a generalization you should be married at 33? That's like looking at somebody who's 70 and saying 'Hey, when are you gonna break your hip? All your friends are breaking their hips – what are you waiting for?'"

— *Sue Kolinsky*

Mastectomy

On learning she needed a mastectomy: "I thought
of the thousands of luncheons and dinners I had
attended where they slapped a name tag on my left
bosom. I always smiled and said, 'Now, what shall
we name the other one?' That would no longer be a
problem."

— *Erma Bombeck*

"A few weeks after my surgery, I went out to play
catch with my golden retriever. When I bent over to
pick up the ball, my prosthesis fell out. The dog
snatched it, and I found myself chasing him down the
road yelling 'Hey, come back here with my breast!'"

— *Linda Ellerbee*

Maturity

"The good thing about going to your twenty-five-
year high school reunion is that you get to see all
your old classmates. The bad thing is that they get
to see you."

— *Anita Milner*

"Old age ain't no place for sissies."

— *Bette Davis*

"I don't know how you feel about old age . . . but in my case I didn't even see it coming. It hit me from the rear."

— *Phyllis Diller*

"Thirty-five is when you finally get your head together and your body starts falling apart."

— *Caryn Leschen*

"Don't think of it as wrinkles. Think of it as relaxed-fit skin."

— *Cathy Crimmins*

"The older I get, the simpler the definition of maturity seems: it's the length of time between when I realize someone is a jackass and when I tell them that they're one."

— *Brett Butler*

"You can't stay young for ever, but you can be immature for the rest of your life."

— *Maxine Wilkie*

"Old age is like a plane flying through a storm. Once you're aboard, there's nothing you can do."

— *Golda Meir*

"The older one grows, the more one likes indecency."

— *Virginia Woolf*

"Don't get upset about wrinkles: they're just foreshadowing."

— *Cathy Crimmins*

Meditation

"I've taken up meditation. I like to have an espresso first to make it more challenging."

— *Betsy Salkind*

Men

"I want a man who's kind and understanding. Is that too much to ask of a millionaire?"
— *Zsa Zsa Gabor*

"Fooling a man ain't all that hard. Finding one that ain't a fool is a lot harder."
— *Gladiola Montana*

"A woman needs a man like a fish needs a net."
— *Cynthia Heimel*

"A man's got to do what a man's got to do. A woman must do what he can't."
— *Rhonda Hansome*

"Why can't men get more in touch with their feminine side and become self-destructive?"
— *Betsy Salkind*

"There's a commercial where guys sit around drinking beer, cleaning fish, wiping their noses on their sleeves and saying 'It doesn't get any better than this.' That's not a commercial. That's a warning."

— *Diane Jordan*

"There are a lot of nice-looking guys out there tonight. But I know no matter how cute and sexy these guys are, there's always someone somewhere who's sick of them."

— *Carol Henry*

"Personally, I think if a woman hasn't met the right man by the time she's twenty-four, she may be lucky."

— *Jean Kerr*

"A good man doesn't just happen. They have to be created by us women. A guy is a lump like a doughnut. So, first you gotta get rid of all the stuff his mom did to him, and then you gotta get rid of all that macho crap that they pick up from the beer commercials. And then there's my personal favourite, the male ego."

— *Roseanne*

"Macho does not prove mucho."

— *Zsa Zsa Gabor*

"It is possible that blondes also prefer gentlemen."

— *Mamie Van Doren*

"A woman is a woman until the day she dies, but a man's a man only as long as he can."

— *Moms Mabley*

"Beware of men who cry. It's true that men who cry are sensitive to and in touch with feelings, but the only feelings they tend to be sensitive to and in touch with are their own."

— *Nora Ephron*

"If they can put one man on the moon why can't they put them all there?"

— *Chocolate Waters*

Q: Can you imagine a world without men?
A: No crime, and lots of happy fat women.

— *Nicole Hollander*

"Men won't stop and ask for directions because driving is too much like sex: they can't stop until they get where they're going."

— *Diane Jordan*

"Men can read maps better than women. 'Cause only the male mind could conceive of one inch equalling a hundred miles."

— *Roseanne*

"Don't accept rides from strange men – and remember that all men are strange as hell."

— *Robin Morgan*

Menstruation

"A guy meets a woman in a bar and wants to take her back to his place. She says, 'I can't, I have my menstrual cycle.' He says, 'That's okay. I'll follow you on my moped.'"

– Bertice Berry

"Every month he asks me if I've got 'the curse'. So, finally, I told him, 'I must. I'm living with you, aren't I?'"

– Stephanie Piro

"I would like it if men had to partake in the same hormonal cycles to which we're subjected monthly. Maybe that's why men declare war – because they have a need to bleed on a regular basis."

– Brett Butler

"Periods are like airplane food. You don't want it, but if yours doesn't come, you go, 'Where's mine?'"

– Bertice Berry

"My doctor said, 'I've got good news and I've got bad news. The good news is you don't have premenstrual syndrome. The bad news is – you're a bitch!'"
— *Rhonda Bates*

"A period is just the beginning of a lifelong sentence."
— *Cathy Crimmins*

Mental health

"Everybody says that having multiple personality disorder is so terrible. I don't think having ninety-two personalities is so terrible. I think it's wonderful because I know so many people who don't even have one."
— *Suzy Berger*

"Co-Dependents' Support Group: 'Let's help each other to stop helping each other!'"
— *Laura Ardiel*

"The statistics on sanity are that one out of every four Americans is suffering from some form of mental illness. Think of your three best friends. If they are okay, then it's you."

— *Rita Mae Brown*

Midlife crisis

"The cup isn't half empty – it's evaporating!"

— *Alice Kahn*

"The mid-life crisis usually begins with a checkup at the doctor's. You feel you are in perfect health. And you are. It's just that you suddenly realize the doctor is some punk kid. You can no longer call him Dr. Silverstein. Instead, you say, 'Do you know a damn thing about systemic yeast, Sean?'"

— *Alice Kahn*

"Menopausal Women Nostalgic For Choice"

— *Bumpersticker*

Mobile homes

"Have you ever noticed that people in mobile home parks never, ever move? I mean look, folks, if you are going to live in the same place for fifty years, get rid of the wheels."

— *Shashi Bhatia*

Money

"Does giving birth make me a real woman? No, earning less than a man makes me a real woman."

— *Suzy Berger*

"I've been sort of crabby lately. It's that time of month again – the rent's due."

— *Margaret Smith*

"At the parking garage the sign says, 'Lost Tickets Pay Max.' What a great deal for Max!"

— *Flash Rosenberg*

"If you are truly serious about preparing your child for the future, don't teach him to subtract – teach him to deduct."

— *Fran Lebowitz*

"I do want to get rich but I never want to do what there is to do to get rich."

— *Gertrude Stein*

"I don't want to make money. I just want to be wonderful."

— *Marilyn Monroe*

"If this man had not twelve thousand a year, he would be a very stupid fellow."

— *Jane Austen*

"I don't buy all this news of a rebounding economy. Just the other day my best friend had a nose job – and twelve people applied."

— *Mary Jo Crowley*

"The most beautiful words in the English language are 'check enclosed'."

— *Dorothy Parker*

"Money is always there, but the pockets change."
— *Gertrude Stein*

Motherhood

"The way I look at it, if the kids are still alive when my husband comes home from work, then I've done my job."

— *Roseanne*

"Never lend your car to anyone to whom you have given birth."

— *Erma Bombeck*

"Children use up the same part of my head as poetry does."

— *Libby Houston*

"I was on a corner the other day when a wild-looking sort of gypsy-looking lady with a dark veil over her face grabbed me right on Ventura Boulevard and said, 'Karen Haber! You're never going to find happiness, and no one is ever going to marry you.' I said, 'Mom, leave me alone.'"

— *Karen Haber*

"My mother says she just wants me to be happy - doing what she wants me to do."

— *Julia Willis*

"I don't have any kids. Well . . . at least none that I know about."

— *Carol Leifer*

"The phrase 'working mother' is redundant."

— *Jane Sellman*

"Never have more children than you have car windows."

— *Erma Bombeck*

"How is a kid going to develop lung power if every little whimper makes Mom come running? My recommendation: keep the baby monitor you got as a gift and put it under the guest bed – lots more fun!"

— *Cathy Crimmins*

"A woman came to ask the doctor if a woman should have children after thirty-five. I said thirty-five is enough for any woman!"

— *Gracie Allen*

"It's not easy being a mother. If it were easy, fathers would do it."

— *Dorothy, 'The Golden Girls'*

"What do you get on Mother's Day if you have kids? You know what. A card with flowers that are made out of pink toilet paper – a lot of pink toilet paper. You get breakfast in bed. Then you get up and fix everybody else their breakfast. And then you go to the bathroom and you are out of toilet paper."

— *Liz Scott*

Movies

"I really detest movies like *Indecent Proposal* and *Pretty Woman* because they send a message to women that sleeping with a rich man is the ultimate goal – and really, that's such a small part of it."
— *Laura Kightlinger*

Music

On Country music: "I love the sound of co-dependence wafting over the prairie."
— *Carol Steinel*

"I worry that the person who thought up Muzak may be thinking up something else."
— *Lily Tomlin*

Optimism

"Hope is the feeling you have that the feeling you have isn't permanent."

— *Jean Kerr*

" 'I'm going to be a big star!' In California, we call that sort of statement 'creative visualization'. In the other forty-nine states, it's called self-delusion."

— *Maureen Brownsey*

People

"There's not much good in the worst of us, and so many of the worst of us get the best of us, that the rest of us aren't even worth talking about."

— *Gracie Allen*

"What are perfect strangers? Do they have perfect hair? Do they dress perfectly?"

— *Ellen Degeneres*

Personal ads

"Personal ads are dangerous. You have to separate the ones who are lying from the ones who are hallucinating."

— *Rita Rudner*

Philosophy

"Sometimes I worry about being a success in a mediocre world."

— *Lily Tomlin*

"Ignorance is no excuse – it's the real thing."

— *Irene Peter*

"If you can keep your head while all about you are losing theirs, it's just possible you haven't grasped the situation."

— *Jean Kerr*

"I had never been as resigned to ready-made ideas as I was to ready-made clothes, perhaps because although I couldn't sew, I could think."

— *Jane Rule*

Politics

"As far as the men who are running for president are concerned, they aren't even people I would date."

— *Nora Ephron*

"A politician is a fellow who will lay down your life for his country."

— *Texas Guinan*

"A female president – maybe they'd start calling it the 'Ova Office'."

— *Brett Butler*

Pregnancy

"If pregnancy were a book, they would cut the last two chapters."

— Nora Ephron

"Pregnancy is much like adolescence, except it's more tiring and you don't get to leave home when it's over."

— Cathy Crimmins

"When I was in labour the nurses would look at me and say, 'Do you still think blondes have more fun?'"

— Joan Rivers

" 'Feel the baby kicking, feel the baby kicking,' says my pregnant friend who is pregnant and deliriously happy about it. To me, life is tough enough without having someone kick you from the inside."

— Rita Rudner

"He tricked me into marrying him. He told me I was pregnant."

— *Carol Leifer*

"I told my mother I was going to have natural childbirth. She said to me, 'Linda, you've been taking drugs all your life. Why stop now?'"

— *Linda Maldonado*

"When I had my baby, I screamed and screamed. And that was just during conception."

— *Joan Rivers*

"If men could get pregnant, abortion would be a sacrament."

— *Flo Kennedy*

When a friend gave birth to a child, Dorothy Parker sent her a congratulatory telegram: "We all knew you had it in you!"

"When I was born, I was so surprised I couldn't talk for a year and a half."

— *Gracie Allen*

"One of my friends told me she was in labour for thirty-six hours. I don't even want to do anything that feels good for thirty-six hours."

— *Rita Rudner*

"One book recommends choosing a Birth Mantra to chant over and over again. I didn't realize until I went into labour that I had subconsciously chosen my mantra: 'Get This Baby Out Of Me.'"

— *Cathy Crimmins*

"The . . . pregnancy bathing . . . suit was the size of a VW beetle, and black with big white polka dots all over it. This swimsuit captured that oh-so-special look at the top of any woman's fashion agenda: Bozo swallows a watermelon."

— *Cathy Crimmins*

Procrastination

"My mother told me, 'Judy, you'll never amount to anything because you always procrastinate.' I said, 'Oh yeah? Just wait!'"

— *Judy Tenuta*

"The only thing that has to be finished by next Tuesday is next Monday."

— *Jennifer Unlimited*

Race & ethnicity

"Jedda is my real name, and Jones is my slave name; it belonged to my ex-husband."

— *Jedda Jones*

"Men look at me and think I'm going to walk on their backs or something. I tell them, 'The only time I'll walk on your back is if there's something on the other side of you that I want.'"

— *Margaret Cho*

"I think we can agree racial prejudice is stupid. Because if you spend time with someone from another race and really get to know them, you can find other reasons to hate them."

— *Bernadette Luckett*

"My mother's Puerto Rican and my father's Russian-Jewish so we consider ourselves to be Jewricans or Puertojews. I think Puertojew sounds like a kosher bathroom, so I prefer Jewrican."

— *Rachel Ticotin*

"I travel a lot, and every day I'm in a different hotel. For some reason, people mistake me for the maid. The other day this guy says, 'You can come into my room and do your job now!' So I went in there and told him some jokes."

— *Bertice Berry*

"There is an incredible amount of magic and feistiness in black men that nobody has been able to wipe out. But everybody has tried."

— *Toni Morrison*

"I don't look like Whoopi Goldberg. People confuse us because we're both black and have dreadlocks. The other day a lady on the bus said to me, 'You look just like Whoopi Goldberg.' I told her, 'You're fat and white, but you don't look like Mama Cass!'"
— *Bertice Berry*

Rage

"Never go to bed mad. Stay up and fight."
— *Phyllis Diller*

"I read one psychologist's theory that said, 'Never strike a child in anger.' When could I strike him? When he's kissing me on my birthday? When he is recuperating from measles? Do I slap the Bible out of his hand on a Sunday?"

— *Erma Bombeck*

Reality

"Every time I close the door on reality it comes in through the windows."

— *Jennifer Unlimited*

"I made some studies, and reality is the leading cause of stress amongst those in touch with it."

— *Jane Wagner*

"In city rooms and in the bars where newspeople drink, you can find out what's going on. You can't find it in the papers."

— *Molly Ivins*

Reincarnation

"You know, I used to believe in reincarnation, but that was in a past life."

— *Karen Salmansohn*

"I don't care about who I was in a former life. Why waste time finding out whether I was Cleopatra or Nefertiti? I believe it's a much better use of time to craft my life in the present ever more passionately. I'd rather work hard to be Flash Rosenberg in Someone Else's former life."

— *Flash Rosenberg*

Religion

"I'm a Catholic. It's a little different being a black Catholic. The name of my church is 'Our Lady Queen of Soul'. We have a big statue of Aretha Franklin in front of the church. She's holding the little baby, Stevie Wonder."

— *Jedda Jones*

"I recently became a Christian Scientist. It was the only health plan I could afford."

— *Betsy Salkind*

"God is love, but get it in writing."

— *Gypsy Rose Lee*

"All religions are the same: religion is basically guilt, with different holidays."

— *Cathy Ladman*

Q: How do you explain human suffering if there is a God?
A: Shouldn't God be the one explaining?

— *Patty Marx*

"When we talk to God, we're praying. When God talks to us, we're schizophrenic."

— *Jane Wagner*

Romance

"Cinderella lied to us. There should be a Betty Ford Center where they deprogram you by putting you in an electric chair, play 'Some Day My Prince Will Come' and hit you and go 'Nobody's coming . . . Nobody's coming . . . Nobody's coming.'"

— *Judy Carter*

"Treat romance like a cane toad. Study it furtively – then squash it!"

– *Kaz Cooke*

Book title: *If You Can't Live Without Me, Why Aren't You Dead Yet?*

– *Cynthia Heimel*

"Remember, lust makes you stupid."

– *Nicole Hollander*

Rules

"If you obey all the rules you miss all the fun."

– *Katherine Hepburn*

Safety

"Advice to children crossing the street: damn the lights. Watch the cars. The lights ain't never killed nobody."

— Moms Mabley

School

"I majored in nursing but I had to drop it because I ran out of milk."

— Judy Tenuta

"Stand firm in your refusal to remain conscious during algebra. In real life, I assure you, there is no such thing as algebra."

— Fran Lebowitz

Science

"The latest scientific studies show that all mice and rats have cancer."

— *Julia Willis*

"The formula for water is H_2O. Is the formula for an ice cube H_2O squared?"

— *Lily Tomlin*

Sex

"What do partners in a co-dependent couple say to each other? 'That was wonderful for you. How was it for me?'"

— *Wendy Kaminer*

"Of course, I'm sure we all place far too much importance on sex, but it's like an old friend of mine used to say: 'When you've seen one, you've seen one.'"

— *Julia Willis*

"Sex is a lot harder for men than women. If a man wants a woman to have sex with him, he's got to ask her out, wine her, dine her, drug her up. . . . But if a woman wants a man to have sex with her, all she has to do is ask for a promotion."

— *Robin Greenspan*

"Some people say older men have long endurance and can make love longer. Let's think about this. Who wants to fuck an old man for a long time?"

— *Marsha Warfield*

"Your daughter is sixteen years old and sexually active? Do I have any advice? For starters — keep her away from Woody Allen!"

— *Lily Tomlin*

"Scientists now say you can get cancer from the radiation thrown off by your electric blanket. I'm so depressed. Here I am fifty-six years old, and the most dangerous thing I've ever done in bed is turn on the blanket."

— *Anita Milner*

"If brevity is the soul of wit, your penis must be a riot."
— *Donna Gephart*

"Freud and Jung broke up over the concept of penis envy. Freud thought that every woman wanted a penis. Jung thought that every woman wanted his penis."
— *Ellen Orchid*

"A hard man is good to find."

— *Mae West*

"I'd get into bondage, but there are too many strings attached."

— *Donna Gephart*

"Sex when you're married is like going to a 7-11. There's not much variety but at three in the morning, it's always there."

— *Carol Leifer*

"Women complain about sex more often than men. Their gripes fall into two major categories: (1) Not enough, (2) Too much."

— *Ann Landers*

"I understand there's a new edition of *Playboy* magazine designed for married men. Every month the centerfold is the same picture."

— *Mary Jo Crowley*

"Nothing was happening in our marriage. I nick-named our waterbed Lake Placid."

— *Phyllis Diller*

About her ex-husband: "In lovemaking, what he lacked in size, he made up for in speed."

— *Roseanne*

"A healthy sex life. Best thing in the world for a woman's voice."

— *Leontyne Price*

"Doctors say it's okay to have sex after a heart attack, provided you close the ambulance door."

— *Phyllis Diller*

"The important thing in acting is to be able to laugh and cry. If I have to cry, I think of my sex life. If I have to laugh, I think of my sex life."

— *Glenda Jackson*

On being told that a new male acquaintance was 6' 7": "Let's forget about the six feet and talk about the seven inches."

— *Mae West*

"My mom always said men are like linoleum floors. Lay 'em right and you can walk all over them for thirty years."

— *Brett Butler*

Q: What do men really like in bed?
A: Breakfast.

— *Nicole Hollander*

"Dr. Ruth says we women should tell our lovers how to make love to us. My boyfriend goes nuts if I tell him how to drive!"

— *Pam Stone*

"You know why God is a man? Because if God was a woman she would have made sperm taste like chocolate."

— *Carrie Snow*

"How lucky we are that we can reach our genitals instead of that spot on our back that itches."

— *Flash Rosenberg*

"If the bedroom were a kitchen, women would be crockpots and men would be microwaves."

— *Diana Jordan*

"If men really knew how to do it, they wouldn't have to pay for it."

— *Roseanne*

Q: Just how responsible am I for my partner's orgasm?

A: Well, I guess that depends on whether or not you're there.

— *Lea Delaria*

"We got new advice as to what motivated man to walk upright: to free his hands for masturbation."

— *Jane Wagner*

"I love the lines men use to get us into bed. 'Please, I'll only put it in for a minute.' What am I, a microwave?"

— *Beverly Mickins*

"He just kept rushing through the lovemaking. Which is the part I like, the beginning part. Most women are like that. We need time to warm up. Why is this hard for you guys to understand? You're the first people to tell us not to gun a cold engine. You want us to go from zero to sixty in a minute. We're not built like that. We stall."

— *Anita Wise*

"I once had a girlfriend who liked sex the best under time pressure – when she had to rush. So we used to pretend that she was an air traffic controller who had ten seconds to come before two jumbo jets would collide in mid-air. That was exciting – the best nine and a half seconds of my life!"

— *Sara Cytron*

Sex education

"I was very sheltered growing up. I knew nothing about sex. My mother said this: 'Sex is a dirty, disgusting thing you save for somebody you love.'"

— *Carol Henry*

"Conservatives say teaching sex education in the public schools will promote promiscuity. With our education system? If we promote promiscuity the same way we promote maths or science, they've got nothing to worry about."

— *Beverly Mickins*

Shopping

"Shopping is better than sex. If you're not satisfied after shopping, you can make an exchange for something you really like."

— *Adrienne Gusoff*

"The only time a woman has a true orgasm is when she's shopping. Every other time she's faking it."

— *Joan Rivers*

"I would rather have a sharp stick in my eye than go shopping."

— *Kate Clinton*

"Buying something on sale is a very special feeling. In fact, the less I pay for something, the more it is worth to me. I have a dress that I paid so little for that I am afraid to wear it. I could spill something on it, and then how would I replace it for that amount of money?"

— *Rita Rudner*

Sleep

"Sleep is death without the responsibility."
— *Fran Lebowitz*

"Can you remember when you didn't want to sleep?
Isn't it inconceivable? I guess the definition of
adulthood is that you want to sleep."
— *Paula Poundstone*

Small towns

"It was such a small town we didn't have a village
idiot. We had to take turns."
— *Billie Holiday*

Smoking

To someone who commented that she couldn't get to heaven with smoke on her breath: "Yes, chile, but when I goes to heaven I expect to leave my breath behind."

— *Sojourner Truth*

Solitude

"I'm single because I was born that way."

— *Mae West*

"One of the advantages of living alone is that you don't have to wake up in the arms of a loved one."

— *Marion Smith*

"We're all in this together – by ourselves."

— *Lily Tomlin*

Space exploration

"I think the space program really needs to be rethought. Our whole approach to space has been very male. We went up to the moon. We walked around on it. And we never came back. We never called. We never wrote. It's the typical one-night stand."

— *Beth Lapides*

Sports

"Golf is not a sport. Golf is men in ugly pants, walking."

— *Rosie O'Donnell*

"My mom said she learned how to swim. Someone took her out in the lake and threw her off the boat and that's how she learned how to swim. I said, 'Mom, they weren't trying to teach you how to swim.'"

— *Paula Poundstone*

"Give a man a fish and you feed him for a day. Teach a man to fish, and you get rid of him on weekends."
— *Nancy Gray*

"Whoever said, 'It's not whether you win or lose that counts,' probably lost."
— *Martina Navratilova*

About football: "You might just as well put in your time watching a lot of ants running in and out of their hole."
— *Lorena Hickok*

"Every time a baseball player grabs his crotch, it makes him spit. That's why you should never date a baseball player."
— *Marsha Warfield*

"Those football players aren't so hot . . . take away the helmets, the shoulder pads, the jerseys, the tight pants – and what do you have? Oh my gosh!"
— *Marie Mott*

Stress

"I read this article. It said the typical symptoms of stress are eating too much, smoking too much, impulse buying, and driving too fast. Are they kidding? This is my idea of a great day!"

— *Monica Piper*

Success

"There is no point at which you can say, 'Well, I'm successful now. I might as well take a nap.'"

— *Carrie Fisher*

Telecommunications

"At the end of every year, I add up the time that I've spent on the phone 'on hold' and subtract it from my age. I don't count that time as really living."

— *Rita Rudner*

"For a list of all the ways technology has failed to improve the quality of life, please press three . . ."

— *Alice Kahn*

"It says a lot about your life what you have on your speed dial. I have two things on mine and I get them confused: the take-out chicken place and the suicide hotline. You don't know what it's like to be bawling your eyes out for twenty minutes and some lady breaks in, 'You want the nine-piece bucket or the twelve-piece bucket?' I don't know how many times I've called the suicide hotline to see what's holding my chicken up."

— *Joan Keiter*

"We don't care. We don't have to. We're the phone company."

— *Lily Tomlin, as Ernestine*

Book title: *Hi. This is Sylvia. I can't come to the phone right now, so when you hear the beep, please hang up.*

— *Nicole Hollander*

"Many are called but few are called back."

— *Mary Tricky*

Television

"The whole world isn't watching anymore – it's renting videos."

— *Julia Willis*

"Television has proved that people will look at anything rather than each other."

— *Ann Landers*

"I'm at a point where I want a man in my life – but not in my house! Just come in, attach the VCR, and get out."

— *Joy Behar*

"My children refused to eat anything that hadn't danced on TV."

— *Erma Bombeck*

"I eat too many TV dinners. I've gotten to the point where every time I see aluminium foil I start to salivate."

— *Ellen Orchid*

Therapy

"I went to a conference for bulimics and anorexics. . . . The bulimics ate the anorexics."

— *Monica Piper*

"The problem with therapy is it takes me more than fifty minutes to calm down enough to get in touch with my anxiety."

— *Lori Sprecher*

"I've been trying to find ways to overcome my inferiority complex. I considered therapy, till I saw the listings in the yellow pages: 'Abusive Relationships', 'Eating Disorders', 'Drug Addiction'. I only have low self-esteem. My problems aren't good enough."

— *Anita Wise*

Time

"The future isn't what it used to be."
— *Linda Moakes*

"I've been on a calendar but never on time."
— *Marilyn Monroe*

Travel

"Is there anything as horrible as starting on a trip? Once you're off, that's all right, but the last moments are earthquake and convulsion, and the feeling that you are a snail being pulled off your rock."
— *Anne Morrow Lindbergh*

"To put it rather bluntly, I am not the type who wants to go back to the land; I am the type who wants to go back to the hotel."
— *Fran Lebowitz*

"You ever hear of Freud airlines? They have two sections. Guilt and non-guilt. The seats go all the way back . . . to childhood."

— *Ellen Orchid*

"I don't mind hecklers. I know how to ignore people. I was an airline stewardess."

— *Joanne Dearing*

"The bus scares me. Sixty-five people on the bus and I was the last one on. I felt like calling *Unsolved Mysteries*. 'Yeah, I found everybody.'"

— *Kathleen Madigan*

Truth

"I never know how much of what I say is true."

— *Bette Midler*

Twins

"We were born ten minutes apart, Adrian first. She always said she was the real baby, and I was a kind of backup."

— *Adair Lara*

Underwear

"What is Victoria's Secret? My guess is that she likes to dress like a slut."

— *Carol Siskind*

"Brevity is the soul of lingerie."

— *Dorothy Parker*

"Like every good little feminist-in-training in the sixties, I burned my bra – and now it's the nineties and I realize Playtex has supported me better than any man I've ever known."

— *Susan Sweetzer*

"My Playtex Living Bra died – of starvation."

— *Phyllis Diller*

"A lady is one who never shows her underwear intentionally."

— *Lillian Day*

"I'll tell you what Victoria's Secret is. The secret is that nobody that's thirty-four inches or thirty-four years can fit into that shit."

— *Mary Ann Nichols*

War

"You can no more win a war than you can win an earthquake."

— *Jeanette Rankin*

"If women ruled the world and we all got massages, there would be no war."

— *Carrie Snow*

"I have just come up with a wonderful solution to end all wars – let men give directions on how to get there."

— *Erma Bombeck*

"Non-violence is a flop. The only bigger flop is violence."

— *Joan Baez*

Weather

"I was really happy when they started naming hurricanes after men. It made national disasters sound even more like my emotional life. 'Brian Wrecks All' could be a headline from my journal."

— *Regina Barreca*

Women

"God made man, and then said I can do better than that and made woman."

— *Adela Rogers St. Johns*

"Any woman who has a great deal to offer the world is in trouble. And if she's a black woman, she's in deep trouble."

— *Hazel Scott*

"A woman without a man is like a fish without a bicycle."

— *Gloria Steinem*

"Calling women the weaker sex makes about as much sense as calling men the stronger one."

— *Gladiola Montana*

"The only problem with women is men."

— *Kathie Sarachild*

" 'Slut' used to mean a slovenly woman. Now it means a woman who will go to bed with everyone. This is considered a bad thing in a woman, although perfectly fabulous in a man. 'Bitch' means a woman who will go to bed with everyone but you."

— *Cynthia Heimel*

"We haven't come a long way, we've come a short way. If we hadn't come a short way, no one would be calling us baby."

— *Elizabeth Janeway*

Work

"To celebrate 'Take Your Daughter To Work Day' this year we're both cleaning out the toilet."

— *Helene Siskind Parsons*

"I think of my boss as a father figure. That really irritates her."

— *Mary Jo Crowley*

"Real equality is going to come not when a female Einstein is recognized as quickly as a male Einstein, but when a female schlemiel is promoted as quickly as a male schlemiel."

— *Bella Abzug*

"The hours are rough in advertising – and in particular here at The Miller Agency. Mike Miller has a saying: if you don't come in on Saturday, don't bother coming in on Sunday."

— *Karen Salmansohn*

"There are very few jobs that actually require a penis or vagina. All other jobs should be open to everybody."

— *Flo Kennedy*

"Adults are always asking little kids what they want to be when they grow up because they're looking for ideas."

— *Paula Poundstone*

"Whatever women must do they must do twice as well as men to be thought half as good. Luckily, this is not difficult."

— *Charlotte Whitton*

Michael O'Mara Humour

If you would like more information on the full list of humour titles published by Michael O'Mara Books Limited please contact our UK sales department by fax on (020) 7622 6956 or email us at: jokes@michaelomarabooks.com.

Titles include:

- *Strange Tails*
- *Wrong!*
- *The Complete Book of Farting*
- *On Second Thoughts*
- *Bitch!*
- *The World's Greatest Lies*
- *The World's Stupidest Signs*
- *The World's Stupidest Laws*
- *Stupid Movie Lines*
- *The Stupidest Things Ever Said*
- *The Stupidest Things Ever Done*
- *Stupid Things Men Do*
- *Stupid Sex*
- *The Nastiest Things Ever Said*
- *The Little Book of Stupid Men*
- *The Little Book of Farting*
- *The Little Book of Venom*
- *The Little Toilet Book*
- *The Little Book of Pants*
- *The Little Book of Pants 2*
- *The Little Book of Blondes*
- *The Little Book of Voodoo*
- *The Little Book of Magical Love Spells*
- *The Little Book of Revenge*
- *The Little Book of Bums*
- *Dot On Top*
- *Dot On Men*
- *Life: an abuser's manual*